# THE
# FILMS
## OF
# STEPHEN
# KING

# THE FILMS OF STEPHEN KING

### ANN LLOYD

BROWN
BOOKS

First published in Great Britain in 1993 by
Brown Books, 255-257 Liverpool Road, London N1 1LX

ISBN 1-897884-06-0

Printed and bound by Ebenezer Baylis & Son, Worcester, UK
Colour origination by Colour Systems, Maidstone, UK

**AUTHOR'S ACKNOWLEDGEMENTS**
I would like to thank Dave Kent for all his sound advice, and for his help as a director
of the Kobal Collection. Thanks, too, to all the staff of the Kobal Collection. I gratefully
acknowledge Alan Jones, editor of the splendid *Shivers* magazine, for permitting the
use of an interview with Fraser Heston, director of *NEEDFUL THINGS*, and for his
knowledgeable contributions to magazines such as *Cinefantastique* and *Starburst*.
Thanks also to Castle Rock and Columbia for providing material, and to all who
assisted me at Brown Packaging.

Finally, thanks to Arnold, K.K. and Efua — always my inspirations.

**BIBLIOGRAPHY**
*The Complete Stephen King Encyclopedia*
by Stephen Spignesi, published by
Contemporary Books Inc. Chicago 1991.
*The Art of Darkness: The Life and Fiction
of the Master of the Macabre* by Douglas
E. Winter, published by New English
Library. Sevenoaks, Kent 1989.
*Bare Bones: Conversations on Terror with
Stephen King* by Tim Underwood and
Chuck Miller, published by McGraw-Hill
Book Company. New York 1988.
*The Stephen King Companion* by George
Beahm, published by Futura (MacDonald
& Co). London 1991.
*Reign of Fear: the Fiction and Films of
Stephen King* edited by Don Herron,
published by Underwood-Miller.
Lancaster, Pennsylvania 1992.
*Stephen King at the Movies* by Jessie
Horsting, published by Starlog Press
Publications. New York 1986.

*Cinefantastique* magazine, Illinois,
Volumes 9, 10, 12, 14, 20, 21, 24.
*Starburst* magazine, London,
June 1984 & April 1991 editions.
*American Film* magazine,
New York, June 1986.
*Shivers* magazine, London,
August 1992 & July 1993 editions.
*What's on in London* magazine,
21-28 September 1988 edition.
*The Independent* newspaper,
26 April 1991.

In addition, much illumination has come
from the words of Stephen King himself,
through many interviews and through his
own splendid treatise on horror,
*Danse Macabre*, published by Futura
(Macdonald & Co). London 1982.

# Contents

# Horror's 'Maine Man'

*'Close all the doors so they can't get out and just scare the hell out of 'em.'*

'**The horror film**', says Stephen King in *Danse Macabre*, his detailed thesis on horror, 'is an invitation to indulge in deviant, antisocial behaviour by proxy — to commit gratuitous acts of violence, indulge our puerile dreams of power, to give in to our most craven fears. Perhaps more than anything else, the horror story or horror movie says it's okay to join the mob, to become the total tribal being, to destroy the outsider.'

Who is this man who will gladly go with you out on the night shift, will be there with you when the clock's hand reaches four past midnight, will go ahead of you into the dead zone — but won't let you pretend you only came during your tea break, or to let your hair down, or just out of idle curiosity? He's the man who knows that you want him to disturb you — to scare you to just this side of a heart attack. His dark side and your shadow have a date with terror.

*'I like to scare people and people like to be scared. That's what I'm here to do.'*

It all began — Stephen Edwin King began — on 21 September, 1947, in Portland Hospital, Maine, at 1.30am. The Moon shone in Sagittarius (helpfully trining Pluto and Saturn aligned in Cancer). His parents were Nellie Ruth and Donald King, and he already had a two-year-old adopted brother called David. Two years later, Donald King went out one night to buy some cigarettes and never reappeared, so Mrs King raised the boys on her own.

The three of them moved around a lot in Stephen's early years, but mostly lived in Maine. Then, in 1958, Mrs King

settled in Durham, Maine, to look after her ailing, elderly parents. Shortly after this Stephen, who had already been writing stories for several years, and Dave found a box of paperbacks that had belonged to their father. It was King's introduction to, among others, H.P. Lovecraft. This discovery was soon followed by horror comics and the fiction of Richard Matheson (the author of the classic horror story *I Am Legend*), whom he credits with having shown him that horror stories don't have to be set in Gothic castles; the monster can be at large on any small-town high street; the person harbouring dark forces may be the mail-man.

King's first published story was 'I Was a Teenage Grave Robber', which appeared in 1965 in *Comics Review* while he was still at high school. He then went on to study at the University of Orono in

■ The face of Stephen King first sprouted to stardom as Jordy Verrill in *CREEPSHOW* (1982). Although critics and viewers found his performance perfectly acceptable, King has since then confined himself to passing through his movies, rather than hanging around in them.

## KING ON 'KING' MOVIES

*'I love the movies, and when I go to see a movie that's been made from one of my books, I know that it isn't going to be exactly like my novel because a lot of other people have interpreted it. But I also know it has an idea that I'll like because that idea occurred to me, and I spent a year, or a year and a half of my life working on it.'*

Maine, and emerged with an English degree and a teaching certificate. He had, while there, contributed a regular column to the college newspaper, published a lot of stories in college literary magazines, written several novels, been politically active, and done a number of jobs to help pay his way through (he was living on the poverty line). The jobs included working in the college library, where he met fellow-student Tabitha Spruce — also destined to be a writer.

*'I find that Stephen really has a direct tap into the thing that really chills us ... Stephen really knows what he's doing. He's the best at that.'*

TOBE HOOPER, DIRECTOR OF *SALEM'S LOT*

On graduation, King was at first unable to find a teaching job, and he worked in an industrial laundry. Eventually (in the fall of 1971) he was hired by Hampton Academy, in Maine. He and Tabitha married, and a daughter, Naomi, followed in due course. (Joe arrived next, and then there was a five-year gap before Owen came along.) King's wages at the time were so low that it was a question of the kids' medicine or the telephone bill, and the phone had to go.

King had had some stories published, mainly by men's magazines (*Cavalier, Adam*). His novels, however, had all been rejected. In desperation, he began reworking and extending a short story, 'Carrie'. At one point he abandoned it, but Tabitha fished it out of the waste-bin and persuaded him to send it to a publisher. It was accepted; an 'advance' cheque of $2500 appeared, and this, his first novel, appeared in the bookshops in 1974.

However, *Carrie* had much more to offer. First, the paperback rights were bought for $400,000. King, who was alone in the house when the news arrived, remembers feeling that he had

to mark the occasion with a present for Tabitha, but all he was able to think of was a hairdryer. The paperback edition of *Carrie* enabled King to give up teaching and begin writing full time. Next came Brian De Palma's film *CARRIE* (1976), which made Stephen King's name known to the cinemago-ing 'masses'. The following year brought him his first hardcover best-seller — *The Shining*.

King was by this time high-profile enough for people to start asking him, 'Why?' Why do you write 'this stuff' (ie horror)? 'What terrible childhood traumas set you upon this strange path, which is no way for a grown man to make a living — never mind, in due course, an absolute fortune?' There possibly was an early trauma, but King doesn't believe that it explains every-thing. His mother tells of his coming home 'white as a ghost' one day when he was very young, and disappearing off to his room. She learned later that one of his friends had been killed (and dismembered) by a freight train, but King himself has no memory of it (although he used the story as an element of 'The Body', filmed as *STAND BY ME* ((1986)).

King explains cheerfully that he has an obsession with the macabre, and that it's 'a marketable obsession'. Furthermore, he maintains, the horror-writer can absorb and relieve you of your fears: 'The tale of monstrosity and terror is a basket loosely packed with

phobias; when the writer passes by, you take one of his imaginary horrors out of the basket and put one of your real ones in it — at least for a time.'

In the process, King says, he manages to exorcise his own fears. What scares him? 'Everything.' This includes: bugs generally but especially spiders, squishy things, snakes, rats, closed-in spaces, getting stuck in elevators, airplanes, deformity, death. The two highest-ranking terrors are probably something terrible happening to his wife and/or children, and The Dark. When he goes to bed, he's very

■ *Opposite*: The success of Brian De Palma's film *CARRIE* (1976) saw the start of the Stephen King phenomenon.
■ *Above Left*: The director George A. Romero (left) with Stephen King on the set of *CREEPSHOW* (1982).
■ *Left*: King in the driving seat as director of *MAXIMUM OVERDRIVE* (1986).

## VIRTUAL UNREALITY

In 1992, a legal storm blew up over a film advertised in the UK as 'Stephen King's *THE LAWNMOWER MAN*'. King had written a story called 'The Lawnmower Man', published in his *Night Shift* collection, about a gardener who powers his mower with his mind, thanks to his master, the Greek god Pan. When the man who hires him complains, he is mown down and becomes Pan's next sacrifice.

Director Brett Leonard took the lawnmower from King's story and gave it to a 'simple' gardener called Jobe Smith (played by Jeff Fahey) who mows the lawn of scientist Lawrence Angelo (Pierce Brosnan). Angelo resigns from his 'Virtual Reality' computer research at Cybertech when the government devises destructive uses for his work. He begins experimenting on Jobe, whose intelligence begins to develop, together with various psychic abilities.

The film boasted a spectacular array of computer graphics, and was a box-office success. It echoed 'King' concepts from *CARRIE*, *FIRESTARTER* and *THE DEAD ZONE*, but bore no resemblance to the story 'The Lawnmower Man'. Back in Maine, Stephen King was not amused. He stipulated that his name be removed from the film, and demanded a percentage of the profits that had accrued from using it. Nevertheless — somewhere — *THE LAWNMOWER MAN 2* is brewing ...

## SURREALLY SCARY

*'I think now that the only place you can write about nice people, nice things, is in the horror story. It's like that painting by Magritte, with the steam engine coming through the fireplace ... because the steam engine is coming through the wall, everything in that room is important.'*

(Stephen King, *The Guardian, May 1983.*)

careful to make sure his legs are under the blankets before the lights go out. If he leaves a leg sticking out, a hand may stretch up to grasp his ankle. He knows the thing under the bed isn't real, but 'I also know that if I'm careful to keep my foot under the covers, it will never be able to grab my ankle.'

■ King on the set of *PET SEMATARY* (1989). The author kept the book in a drawer for a long time, so disturbing did he find this story of a child who returns, gruesomely character-changed, from the dead. In the film King has a role as the minister who leads the service at the kid's funeral.

But while King is writing, and thereby serving an important social function, and saving himself a fortune in psychiatry fees, something else is also going on: he's enjoying himself! He knows how to scare people, how to get under their skin, and he loves to do it — any way he can. 'I will try to terrorize the reader. But if I find I cannot terrify him/her, I will try to horrify. And if I find I cannot horrify, I'll go for the gross-out! I'm not proud.'

King has now sold hundreds of millions of books and tens of millions

*'I'm usually writing with a great big grin on my face.'*

of cinema tickets. He is the most popular horror-fiction writer that has ever lived. In 1992 he was listed as the world's 29th highest-earning entertainer (one above Mel Gibson), and had made over $20 million in the previous two years.

When it comes to horror fiction, King himself agrees he is a brand name 'like a Big Mac'. However, the Stephen King phenomenon has not been lightly achieved. King writes at least two hours a day, seven days a week and 362 days a year. A good many more

■ The State of Maine is a subject very close to King's heart. Whenever possible, he stipulates that some or all of the filming of his stories should be done there. *GRAVEYARD SHIFT* (1990) was filmed entirely in and around his home town of Bangor, Maine.

daily hours are spent reading, musing, and toying with ideas. Apart from his skills as a horrormeister, King is widely acclaimed as a chronicler of middle-Americana. He has been described as a 'noticer'; it is his extraordinary attention to the details of everyday life which enables him to create characters that everyone is able to identify with, in a situation that's as homely as apple pie — until it just tips over into unimaginable horror.

The first movie Stephen King remembers seeing is *CREATURE FROM THE BLACK LAGOON* (1954). Movies were an important part of his childhood; and today, his is the name that can be found above the title of a not insignificant number. Some movie versions of his books he has enjoyed enormously. Of others he says, 'There is no movie that can ruin a book. They can embarrass a writer — sort of like showing up at a party with your fly open — but these things pass, while the books remain.'

Does he have any remaining ambitions? 'I suppose the ultimate triumph would be to have somebody drop dead of a heart attack. I'd say "Gee, that's a shame," and I'd mean it, but part of me would be thinking, "Jesus, that really worked!"'

## KING ON 'KING' MOVIES

'To a lot of people in Hollywood ... the stuff I've written is extremely visual. It looks like it comes to them and it begs to be made into a movie ... It might be that they feel too much of it is there to start with and they don't have to work on it hard enough. I think that it's tough to break the gap between the warmth in the novel that makes the characters seem worth loving and caring about, set off against the horrors. When they make the movie they concentrate on the moment when the monster comes out and starts waving his claws. I don't think that's what people are interested in.'

*From an interview with Stephen King by Gary Wood, Cinefantastique magazine, February 1991.*

■ Cats play a significant role in King's movies. In *SLEEPWALKERS* (1992) cat-mutants are the villains, whereas moggies, led by Clovis (left, with King) are the film's heroes.

# Carrie 1976

*'Behold I was shapen in wickedness: and in sin hath my mother conceived me.'*

(THE BOOK OF COMMON PRAYER)

**DIRECTOR:**
**Brian De Palma**
*(USA, 1976)*

**LEADING PLAYERS:**
**Sissy Spacek** (Carrie White), **Piper Laurie** (Margaret White), **Amy Irving** (Sue Snell), **William Katt** (Tommy Ross), **John Travolta** (Billy Nolan), **Nancy Allen** (Chris Hargenson), **Betty Buckley** (Miss Collins), **P.J. Soles** (Norma Watson), **Sydney Lassick** (Mr Fromm), **Stefan Gierasch** (Principal Morton), **Priscilla Pointer** (Mrs Snell), **Michael Talbot** (Freddy), **Noelle North** (Freida), **Cameron De Palma** (boy on bicycle).

**PRODUCTION COMPANY:**
**Red Bank Films**

**PRODUCER:**
**Paul Monash**

**SCREENPLAY:**
**Lawrence D. Cohen**; based on the novel by **Stephen King.**

Photographer: **Mario Tosi.** Editor: **Paul Hirsch.** Art directors: **William Kenny, Jack Fisk.** Sound: **Bertil Hallberg.** Music: **Pino Donaggio.** Costume designer: **Rosanna Norton.** Make-up: **Wesley Dawn.** Special effects: **Gregory M. Auer.** Stunt co-ordinator: **Richard Weiker.** Colour: **MGM**; prints by **DeLuxe.**

**RUNNING TIME:**
**97 mins**

## SYNOPSIS

Carrie White, shy and socially backward at school, freaks out in the showers when she starts to 'bleed'. The gym mistress rescues her from her jeering classmates and punishes them. Sue, one of her classmates, is remorseful, and persuades her boyfriend, Tommy, to take Carrie to the Senior Prom. Chris, the cruellest of the girls, is banned from the Prom and plans a vicious revenge.

Carrie goes home to her mother, Margaret, who locks her in a cupboard to pray for her 'sins', and forbids her to go to the Prom. But Carrie's traumas have triggered her telekinetic powers, and she uses them to keep her mother at bay while she dresses for her date. Once at the dance, she and Tommy are voted King and Queen of the Prom.

However, the ballot has been rigged by Chris, who has also rigged up a booby trap. As Carrie receives her trophy, she is drenched by a bucketful of pig's blood. In a teleki-netic rage, she locks the school doors and sets the building alight, burning to death all those inside. Chris and her boyfriend Billy escape, but Carrie fatally crashes their car before she returns home. There, her mother stabs her, believing her to be devil-possessed. Carrie 'projects' a lethal barrage of kitchen knives at Margaret, and then burns the house down around them both.

For Sue, who escaped the school conflagration, the guilt is unending — and the nightmares unceasing.

---

***CARRIE*** opens with a high overhead shot of a girls' school volleyball game. The camera zooms in to find Carrie, just in time to witness her missing her shot and losing the game for her team. The comments of her team-mates, as they sweep past her on the way to the locker-room, are angry and disdainful. Once inside, Carrie surrenders herself to the simple pleasure of soaping her body under a warm shower; but then the streaming water turns bright red — blood is pouring from her.

Shock, horror! Carrie has started to menstruate (very late, if she's about to go to her Senior Prom) — and right in front of the camera! In reaction to the trauma of this event — worsened by her classmates' reaction (they pelt her with tampons and chant 'Plug it up!'), Carrie's telekinetic powers emerge, and her anger and fear cause the locker-room light bulb to explode.

Several of De Palma's movie themes have now been set: when trouble is 'hovering', the camera moves in on an overhead shot; when Carrie gets upset, things begin to blow; and rivers of blood will flow before this rites-of-passage tale is at an end.

King says he's always seen *Carrie*, the novel, as a parable of women's consciousness. It also, he observes, says a great deal about men's fears — '... about menstruation and about dealing with women who eat you up'. De Palma certainly went for a landmark depiction, in DeLuxe detail, of menstruation on the cinema screen, shockingly intruding it into a scene of soft sensuality. Both the book and the film also offer, in Carrie's telekinesis, an equally vivid account of how women find their own channels of power.

On Carrie's arrival at home we meet the reason for her sexual ignorance and social ineptitude — her mother. Margaret White once committed a dreadful sin [s-x] and, as a result, Carrie was born and Margaret was 'white' no longer. She has filled her life with atonement: her days are spent bible thumping, and her home is a candlelit mausoleum of religious artefacts. So severe is Margaret's fanaticism that, by the film's end, she has concluded (after witnessing Carrie's devil-sent powers) that her only way to salvation is to return to the time before Carrie was born; so she dons a white 'wedding' gown — and lies in wait to murder her

daughter. The scales, with daughter's sexual repression in one pan, and mother's — compounded into religious fanaticism — in the other, are immaculately balanced. De Palma makes us wait to see which way they will eventually swing.

Back at the school, De Palma is building up to his bucket-of-blood climax. Carrie has transformed herself into a perfect high-school princess, sheathed in pink satin with smooth golden tresses and Maybelline make-up, and she and sports-hero Tommy swirl around on the dance floor in an endless moment of enchantment. Then, as the blood falls and Carrie's wrath rises, De Palma floods the scene with a red filter, and he employs a

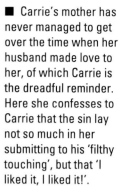

■ Carrie's mother has never managed to get over the time when her husband made love to her, of which Carrie is the dreadful reminder. Here she confesses to Carrie that the sin lay not so much in her submitting to his 'filthy touching', but that 'I liked it, I liked it!'.

■ Carrie is deeply suspicious of Tommy's friendly advances in the library. He's never chatted to her before, and now he's asking her to the school Prom. And everyone knows this track-and-field ace doesn't read books!

■ Billy Nolan has no particular quarrel with Carrie, but he helps his girlfriend Chris to rig up the bucket of pig's blood that will soak Carrie. He then tries to run her down, so he will have to pay ...

multiple split screen in order to depict all of the lethal effects of Carrie's blazing ire simultaneously.

The book, says King, 'tries to deal with the loneliness of one girl, her desperate effort to become a part of the peer society in which she must exist, and how her efforts fail. If it had any thesis to offer, it was that high school is a place of almost bottomless conservatism and bigotry...'

Sue, the classmate who was ashamed of having taunted Carrie, and who sacrificed her Prom night (and her boyfriend) in penance, is allowed to remain. But it seems that Carrie hasn't forgiven her, and exacts another piece of vengeance that generates one of cinema history's all-time-great seat-leaving moments.

Of the many movie adaptations of Stephen King's novels and stories, *CARRIE* is one of those that provides most of his fans with a good deal of satisfaction. Although De Palma changes the structure of the book for his film (the book's story is told through a series of reports, newspaper cuttings and second-hand accounts, most of which are attempting to make sense of the bizarre occurrences surrounding Carrie White), he takes care to encapsulate the very essence of the type of small-town restrictions and hypocrisies which tend to breed 'Margaret Whites'.

Many of the later film adaptations that were made of King's work sacrificed too many details of character and setting in order to leave maximum room for the horror effects.

## CARRIE – OKAY

*CARRIE* was an enormous success. It confirmed the prodigious talent of the director Brian De Palma, who had hitherto been regarded as 'promising' but rather derivative (especially of Alfred Hitchcock) in his previous excursions into horror movies. It put 'on the map' several young stars-to-be who had only had, at most, bit parts before: Nancy Allen (shortly after to marry De Palma), Amy Irving (later to marry Steven Spielberg), William Katt (who shone quite brightly for a while) and John Travolta. And although Sissy Spacek (already married to John Fisk, one of *CARRIE*'s art directors) had been critically acclaimed in *BADLANDS* (1973), it was *CARRIE* which launched her movie career. It re-launched the career of Piper Laurie, who had been away from filming for 15 years — since her starring role opposite Paul Newman in *THE HUSTLER* (1961). Both Laurie and Spacek were Oscar-nominated for *CARRIE*.

The other career that *CARRIE* launched was that of a little-known writer called Stephen King. Although King had had many stories published, *Carrie* was his first novel, and so 'little-known' was he that the publishers didn't bother to put his name on the book's front cover. When the film appeared, the critics regarded it merely as a De Palma movie; neither the novel nor King was worth a mention. However, after the film's release the paperback version of *Carrie* was published, with a picture of Sissy Spacek on the cover — and, in large letters, 'Stephen King'.

■ A girl who's mad, as mad as hell! Carrie, drenched in the pig's blood, almost floats home from school on her anger, before deflating into the abject misery of her loneliness, her rejection, her humiliation and her mother.

## KING ON CARRIE

'Brian De Palma's CARRIE was terrific. He handled the material deftly and artistically, and got a fine performance out of Sissy Spacek. In many ways the film is far more stylish than my book, which I still think is a gripping read but is impeded by a certain heaviness ... a quality that's absent from the film ...'

(From an interview with Stephen King, by Eric Norden, published in US Playboy, June 1983.)

# The Shining 1980

DIRECTOR:
**Stanley Kubrick**
*(GB, 1980)*

LEADING PLAYERS:
**Jack Nicholson** (Jack Torrance), **Shelley Duvall** (Wendy Torrance), **Danny Lloyd** (Danny Torrance), **Scatman Crothers** (Hallorann), **Barry Nelson** (Ullman), **Phillip Stone** (Grady), **Joe Turkel** (Lloyd), **Anne Jackson** (doctor), **Tony Burton** (Durkin), **Lia Beldam** (young woman in bathtub), **Billie Gibson** (old woman in bathtub), **Lisa Burn** and **Louise Burn** (Grady girls), **Norman Gay** (Axe Head — injured guest).

PRODUCTION COMPANY:
**Hawk Films**

PRODUCER:
**Stanley Kubrick**

SCREENPLAY:
**Stanley Kubrick, Diane Johnson**; based on the novel by **Stephen King**.

Photographer: **John Alcott**.
Editor: **Ray Lovejoy**.
Production designer: **Roy Walker**. Art director: **Les Tomkins**. Costume designer: **Milena Canonero**.
Art director: **Les Tomkins**.
Make-up: **Tom Smith, Barbara Daly**.
Sound: **Ivan Sharrock, Richard Daniel**. Music: **Wendy Carlos, Bela Bartok, Krysztof Penderecki, Gyorgy Ligeti, Rachel Elkin, Henry Hall**. Colour.

RUNNING TIME:
**146 mins**
(later cut to 119 mins)

*A whole winter spent in a luxury hotel. Was ever a family so lucky?*

The tide of terror that swept America IS HERE

**THE SHINING** X

A STANLEY KUBRICK FILM JACK NICHOLSON SHELLEY DUVALL "THE SHINING" SCATMAN CROTHERS DANNY LLOYD STEPHEN KING STANLEY KUBRICK & DIANE JOHNSON STANLEY KUBRICK JAN HARLAN THE PRODUCER CIRCLE CO.

## SYNOPSIS

Jack Torrance, an ex-teacher who has ambitions to write a novel, takes a job at the huge Overlook Hotel up in the Rockies. Jack is to be caretaker during the winter months when the hotel is closed and snowed-in, and he and wife Wendy and small son Danny arrive as the staff are packing to leave.

The hotel's cook, Hallorann, realizes that Danny has what his grandmother called 'the shining' — the gift of both clairvoyance and telepathy. Danny has already had scary 'flashes' from the hotel, and didn't want to come, but soon he is pedalling up and down the hotel corridors on his tricycle, while Wendy prepares meals in the huge kitchens and Jack types away at his novel. Jack, who rapidly turns manically moody, has been told that the previous caretaker had 'flipped' and axe-murdered his twin daughters before shooting himself.

The spectres of these and other of the hotel's past inmates begin to appear to Jack and Danny. The ghost of the previous caretaker, Grady, tells Jack that he, too, must 'correct' his wife and child. Jack goes after Wendy with an axe, but she contrives to lock him in a storeroom. Danny sends a telepathic SOS to Hallorann in Florida. Hallorann immediately sets out on a rescue bid. He struggles to reach the hotel, through a blizzard, by snowmobile, but on arrival he is killed by Jack who has been released by Grady. Jack chases Danny through the blizzard into the hotel's garden maze, but Danny and Wendy manage to escape in Hallorann's snowmobile, leaving Jack in the maze — where he dies from the cold.

**B**y the time of *THE SHINING*, director Stanley Kubrick was already an enigma to be reckoned with. His CV contained a list of films that had impressed and/or puzzled critics and moviegoers, including *DR STRANGELOVE* (1963), *2001: A SPACE ODYSSEY* (1969), *A CLOCKWORK ORANGE* (1971), *BARRY LYNDON* (1975). Not a lot there to make one think of Kubrick, when searching for his next subject, waving aloft Stephen King's *The Shining* and shouting 'This is it!'. But that was it.

*THE SHINING* deeply divided critical opinion on its opening. Much of the argument centred around Jack Nicholson's no-holds-barred performance. Some couldn't believe that Kubrick would do 40 or 50 takes of each shot (a normal tally for Kubrick) only to have Nicholson produce a steadily more insane grin. Others

■ The Torrance family on their way to spend winter at the Overlook Hotel. Even at this stage Wendy looks worried, Danny looks lonely, and Jack looks as if someone else is already in the driving seat.

insisted that the seeming obviousness of Nicholson's approach was, in fact, devastatingly subtle. For many, one of Kubrick's main sins of omission lay in failing to show how the evil power of the hotel disintegrated a weak but initially sane man; Nicholson's Torrance, they felt, was clearly demented from the word go.

Some couldn't see why Stanley Kubrick would take a book like *The Shining* and, from their point of view, discard all its virtues. Others insisted that in zooming in on the elements of his choice, Kubrick had created a new form of the horror genre — the first epic horror film.

There were those who believed that Kubrick sacrificed characterization to atmosphere, and others who felt that, in this film, the role of the characters was not to develop, but merely to interact with the circumstances.

All were agreed, however, that this was Kubrick's *THE SHINING* and not King's. And all were agreed that Kubrick once again revealed himself to be a master technician and a superb visual artist, and that his and Diane Johnson's script (Kubrick didn't wish to use King's own script) had been filmed with awesome style.

Kubrick made extensive use throughout of the Steadicam, a recently developed gyroscopic mount-

ing which enabled the camera to move far more freely and smoothly than ever before. It was the Steadicam, filming from only a few inches above floor level, that followed little Danny as he tricycled around the hotel, up and down corridors, swishing softly over carpets, and bumping loudly over wooden floors.

It was the Steadicam which glided before the crazed, limping figure of Torrance, axe in hand; and which raced round the snow-covered maze with Danny as he fled from his father — and the axe.

■ At the Overlook Wendy has to cope with a husband who's losing his marbles and a small son who's being terrorized both by ghosts that she can't see and by his psychic 'understanding' of what fate has in store for them.

Danny's role had shifted off-centre from book to film. Nevertheless it is still Danny who first connects with the hotel's murderous forces before the family even arrives there. And it is

Danny who is first contacted by the Overlook's time-warped 'occupants'; the two little Grady girls appear and invite him to play with them — before turning into mutilated apparitions.

Did Kubrick retain any of King's horror in his version? Not much, but he did create some powerful horror of his own. There is a moment of pure terror when Wendy, forbidden to look at Jack's manuscript, but unable to resist, discovers that the only words Jack has written are 'All work and no play makes Jack a dull boy' — over and over and over again.

There are moments when the walls bleed, and when a sea of blood gushes from an elevator. There is Jack's encounter with a beautiful, naked seductress in the forbidden Room 237, only to have her turn into a pustulating cadaver in his arms.

There is the shock of Hallorann's receiving this image, a thousand miles away in Florida, when it is 'beamed' to him from the hotel by Danny. And there is also the building terror of the

■ The Overlook fulfils, for Jack, the dream of every man with an alcohol problem who is living in a 'dry' hotel: a barman who materializes from time to time, complete with bar, and refuses to allow him to pay for his drinks.

## HEARTBREAK HOTEL

The camera helicopters in — a breathtaking shot of a lake and the Colorado Rocky Mountains. It picks up, on a winding mountain road, a small yellow car. It follows the car, carrying Jack Torrance, up to the resort where Torrance has an interview for the job of winter caretaker. And, in cinemas all over the globe, viewers' eyes opened a bit wider as they fastened on the unexpected magnificence of the Overlook Hotel.

Jack enters the palatial reception area. It is the audience's first introduction to the building's vast scale.

Kubrick modelled the Overlook's facade on the Timberland Hotel in Oregon. However, the film was not shot in Oregon, but at Elstree Studios, just outside of London, England. Although principal photography was scheduled for 17 weeks, the vast amount of construction work involved meant that *THE SHINING* occupied the Studios from May 1978 to April 1979. There, Kubrick and production designer Roy Walker created the bedrooms, the ballroom, the lounges, the lobbies, the bathrooms, the corridors, the cupboards, the huge kitchens and their storage rooms, the elevators and the staircases of the Overlook Hotel. Roy Walker then added the opulence, the lush decadence: the huge curving bar, the chandeliers, the gold wallpaper, the gigantic chess set and the miles of carpet. In addition, on another stage, Walker built the whole of the hedge-maze, adjacent to the hotel, in which *THE SHINING*'s final climactic scene takes place.

And there the Overlook sat, on the site of an old Indian burial ground, empty of cooks and barmen and summer vacationers, waiting for Jack Torrance to join its real 'staff'; waiting for Danny Torrance to give it his 'shining' .....

## KING ON THE SHINING

'Stanley Kubrick's version of THE SHINING is a lot tougher for me to evaluate [than CARRIE], because I'm still profoundly ambivalent about the whole thing. I'd admired Kubrick for a long time and had great expectations for the project, but I was deeply disappointed in the end result. Parts of the film are chilling, charged with a relentlessly claustrophobic terror, but others fall flat.

'Kubrick just couldn't grasp the sheer inhuman evil of the Overlook Hotel. So he looked, instead, for evil in the characters and made the film into a domestic tragedy with only vaguely supernatural overtones. That was the basic flaw: because he couldn't believe, he couldn't make the film believable to others ....

'The real problem is that Kubrick set out to make a horror movie with no apparent understanding of the genre.

'Everything about it screams that from beginning to end ....'

*(From an interview with Stephen King, by Eric Norden, published in US* Playboy *June 1983.)*

inevitable: that Jack will follow the hotel's 'orders' and will murder his family — just as his predecessor caretaker Grady had done in his time.

At the end of the movie, with Wendy and Danny snowmobiling to safety, with Hallorann murdered in his attempt to rescue them, and Jack frozen in the maze, the closing shot is of a photograph, taken in the 1920s in the hotel's heyday, showing Jack as the caretaker — safely absorbed into the Overlook's own evil time-zone.

And there the hotel lay, buried for the winter in the snow, but otherwise in the same unfathomable condition it had been in when the Torrances arrived: not a dust sheet anywhere.

■ After pursuing his terrified son at murderous speed through hedged corridors Jack dies because the Overlook forgot to programme in 'the knowledge' of how to get out of the maze.

# Creepshow 1982

DIRECTOR:
**George A. Romero**
*(USA, 1982)*

LEADING PLAYERS:
*WRAP-AROUND STORY*:
**Iva Jean Saraceni** (Billy's
Mother), **Joe King** (Billy),
**Tommy Atkins** (Billy's
Father), **Marty Schiff** (1st
garbageman), **Tom Savini**
(2nd garbageman).
*FATHER'S DAY*:
**Carrie Nye** (Aunt Sylvia
Grantham), **Viveca
Lindfors** (Aunt Bedelia),
**Elizabeth Regan** (Cass
Blaine), **Ed Harris** (Hank
Blaine), **Warner Shook**
(Richard Grantham), **Jon
Lormer** (Nathan
Grantham), **John Amplas**
(Nathan Grantham's
corpse), **Nann Mogg** (Mrs
Danvers), **Peter Messer**
(Yarbro).
*THE LONESOME DEATH
OF JORDY VERRILL*:
**Stephen King** (Jordy
Verrill), **Bingo O'Malley**
(Jordy's father).
*SOMETHING TO TIDE
YOU OVER*:
**Leslie Nielsen** (Richard
Vickers), **Gaylen Ross**
(Becky Vickers), **Ted
Danson** (Harry
Wentworth).
*THE CRATE*:
**Hal Holbrook** (Henry
Northrup), **Adrienne
Barbeau** (Wilma
Northrup), **Fritz Weaver**
(Professor Dexter
Stanley), **Don Keefer**
(Mike the janitor), **Robert
Harper** (Charlie
Gereson), **Cletus
Anderson** (host), **Katie
Karlowitz** (maid), **Chuck
Aber** (Richard Raymond),
**Christine Forrest** (Tabitha
Raymond).
*THEY'RE CREEPING UP
ON YOU*:
**E.G. Marshall** (Upson
Pratt), **David Early** (Mr
White).

*'Tales that will bring you face to face with your deepest fears and nightmares.'*

## SYNOPSIS

Based on a number of short stories by King, *CREEPSHOW* holds all of them together by using a wrap-around story.

**WRAP-AROUND STORY**: Young Billy is deeply engrossed in his precious *Creepshow* horror comic book when his mean ol' Dad snatches it from him and throws it out of the window. To Billy's delight, a gruesome, grinning spectre appears at the window, and beckons to where the book lies in the garbage can. It flutters open to reveal:

**FATHER'S DAY**: 'I want my caaaaake....' were the last words, seven years ago on Father's Day, of demanding parent Nathan Grantham, before he was lethally clouted by his repressed daughter. Now, every Father's Day, the family gather to celebrate his demise. But this year, father comes back to collect his cake.

**THE LONESOME DEATH OF JORDY VERRILL**: When country-bumpkin farmer Jordy sees a meteor land in his field, he figures he ought to be able to sell it for a few bucks. However, the meteor splits in his hand, oozing green 'goo' all over him, which begins to sprout a strange, lurid-green plant-like growth over Jordy, his beer-bottle, his tongue, everything.

**THE CRATE**: Henpecked, cheated-on Professor Henry Northrup learns of something very large, ancient, evil and alive in a 150-year-old crate, and realizes that many of his problems can be solved by introducing 'The Crate' to his shrew of a wife.

**SOMETHING TO TIDE YOU OVER**: TV producer Richard Vickers takes revenge on his cheating wife and her lover by burying them up to their necks in the sand at low tide. He provides them with video screens, so they can watch each other drown. Next day, on his return to the beach, Vickers finds no trace of the bodies — they find him!

**THEY'RE CREEPING UP ON YOU**: Upson Pratt, a ruthless, reclusive, phobia-ridden millionaire, secludes himself safely away in his auto-mated, bug-proof penthouse until the day a power failure finds him alone with cockroaches creeping in through every crack and drainpipe.

**WRAP-AROUND STORY**: Upstairs Billy stabs something with a pin, over and over again. Downstairs Billy's father has agonising aches and pains. Outside the garbagemen find a comic book — and notice an ad for a voodoo doll is cut out....

**The film** *CREEPSHOW* was hailed with enthusiasm by horror-movie buffs as the meeting of three great Modern Masters of the Macabre: the writer Stephen King, the director George A. Romero, and the make-up special-effects maestro Tom Savini.

King and Romero had met one another when Warner Bros. asked Romero if he would like to direct King's novel *Salem's Lot*. Romero bowed out when Warner Bros. decided to make the book into a TV-mini-series instead of a feature film, but by then he and King had discovered they were mutual fans, had become good friends, and resolved to work together in the future.

They finally came up with the idea that they wanted. *CREEPSHOW* was to be an anthology of stories which would be a tribute to the horror comics of the 1950s that they had both known and loved as kids — comics such as *The Vault of Horror* and *Tales From the Crypt*. These comics were

■ For the creature in *THE CRATE*, make-up F/X expert Tom Savini created a hideous concoction of hair, teeth and claws, equipping it with the technology it needed to slurp, snarl and sneer.

pronounced 'trash' and were banned from the house by parents — something that made them all the more loved and cherished.

Yet, however ghoulish, the stories always followed a strong moral code: the bad guys might have had most of the fun, but the good guys won in the end — or at least had their revenge, even if they had to come mouldrin' back from the grave to get it.

Romero, director of such cult classics as *NIGHT OF THE LIVING DEAD* (1968) and *DAWN OF THE DEAD* (1979), had got used to working on his own scripts, but in this case he was happy to let King provide the screenplay (King's first to be produced). He found King very amenable to changes; indeed, as often as not King would spot the need for them first.

Romero sought out a team that could help bring the spirit of the horror comics alive for *CREEPSHOW*. Lighting was specially designed to reproduce the comics' vivid primary colours; this worked so well, and produced, for instance, such garish green vegetation for *JORDY VERRILL* that their problem lay in persuading the lab technicians not to colour-correct.

PRODUCTION COMPANY:
**Laurel Show, Inc.**

PRODUCER:
**Richard P. Rubinstein**

SCREENPLAY:
**Stephen King**. *THE CRATE* is based on King's story *The Crate*. *THE LONESOME DEATH OF JORDY VERRILL* on *Weeds*.

Photographer: **Michael Gornick**. Editors: **Michael Spolan** (*FATHER'S DAY, THEY'RE CREEPING UP ON YOU*), **Pasquale Buba** (*THE LONESOME DEATH OF JORDY VERRILL*), **George A. Romero** (*SOMETHING TO TIDE YOU OVER*), **Paul Hirsch** (*THE CRATE*). Production designer/ scenic special effects: **Cletus Anderson**. Sound: **Pam De Metrius**. Music: **John Harrison**. Costume designer: **Barbara Anderson**. Make-up special effects: **Tom Savini**. Colour.

RUNNING TIME:
**123 mins**

## KING IN CREEPSHOW

■ King's first major screen appearance (in *JORDY VERRILL*) posed a classic method-actor's dilemma: should he portray the transformed Jordy as a walking, talking pot-plant, or as an E.T. weed?

*CREEPSHOW* brought Stephen King his first starring role. Jordy Verrill is two sandwiches short of a picnic, but just bright enough to realise that a meteor in the garden could be worth cash in the hand. He throws water over it to cool it down, but this triggers into action some outerspace seedlings that infest the Verrill place — and Verrill.

Romero had explained to King that the expression he was aiming for was the one to be found in any 'Road Runner' cartoon on the face of the coyote after he realizes that it's five seconds since he ran over the edge of the cliff....

Producer Richard Rubinstein commented: 'Steve turned out to be much more than competent; he gave the role a life of its own.'

King's view of movie stardom was: 'I didn't care for it that much .... Near the end of Jordy I was in a chair for six hours a day getting this Astro-turf stuff put all over my body.'

The little boy who owns the forbidden *Creepshow* comic is none other than Stephen King's son, Joe. Romero spotted a close resemblance between Joe and the face that had been used on the film's promotional poster. Joe read well for the part, and Romero decided he'd be great in it. Said his father: 'Jody did have a good time making *CREEPSHOW*, but he did get freaked out for a while. He was eight or nine at the time, and to be in your pyjamas with a whole bunch of people around your bed in a strange house can be very unsettling. He just came to a point where it was either freak out or go to work. He went to work.'

*(Stephen King quotes from an interview by Edwin Pouncy, published in* Sounds, *May 1983.)*

■ Nathan Grantham, dead some seven years, pays a Father's Day visit to his family. If you think daughter Bedelia got a rough welcome, wait till you see what he did to Sylvia!

correct. The stories were linked by ads (animated for the movie) for jokes, tricks, body-building books and gadgets which would have appeared in horror comics. The opening and closing shots of each story dissolved in or out of the artwork on the relevant comic-book page.

Make-up-effects artist Tom Savini had already worked with Romero on *KNIGHTRIDERS* (1981), as well as creating a plethora of gory effects for the zombie inhabitants of Romero's *DAWN OF THE DEAD*. *CREEPSHOW* necessitated the full spectrum of his talents: the 7-years-buried Nathan (*FATHER'S DAY*), with Sylvia's head adorning his overdue cake; the extra-terrestrial grass that can find nowhere on Jordy Verrill that it doesn't want to grow; the long-toothed, long-clawed monster from *THE CRATE*; the soggy spectres from *SOMETHING TO TIDE YOU OVER*; Pratt's cockroach-ravaged body in *THEY'RE CREEPING UP ON YOU*; together with the menacing

figure of The Creep itself who is putting on the entire show for Billy.

The cast performed their roles with gusto, and the crew joined in: production designer Cletus Anderson pops up in *THE CRATE*; Tom Savini appears as a garbagemen at the movie's end.

■ The Spectre for *CREEPSHOW* was built around a real human skeleton.

## KING ON CREEPSHOW

*'George [Romero] is a director who cares about words. There's a chance to do things in this movie with dialogue that nobody's really cared to do in a horror movie before.'*

*'I'm happy with CREEPSHOW because I was involved with the entire thing from beginning to end, and the writing process was original.'*

*On JORDY VERRILL:*

*'If I had written it for myself, I would have put in at least one sex scene!'*

## The Films of Stephen King

# Cujo 1983

DIRECTOR:
**Lewis Teague**
*(USA, 1983)*

LEADING PLAYERS:
**Dee Wallace** (Donna Trenton), **Daniel Hugh-Kelly** (Vic Trenton), **Danny Pintauro** (Tad Trenton), **Christopher Stone** (Steve Kemp), **Ed Lauter** (Joe Camber), **Kaiulani Lee** (Charity Camber), **Billy Jacoby** (Brett Camber), **Mills Watson** (Gary Previer), **Sandy Ward** (Sheriff Bannerman), **Jerry Hardin** (Masen), **Merritt Olsen** (Professor), **Arthur Rosenberg** (Roger Breakstone), **Harry Donovan-Smith** (Harry), **Robert Elross** (Meara), **Robert Behling** (Fournier), **Claire Nono** (lady reporter), **Daniel H. Blatt** (Dr Merkatz).

PRODUCTION COMPANY:
**Taft Entertainment Company**

PRODUCERS:
**Daniel H. Blatt**, **Robert Singer**

SCREENPLAY:
**Don Carlos Dunaway**, **Lauren Currier**; based on the novel by **Stephen King**.

Photographer: **Jan De Bont**. Editor: **Neil Travis**. Production designer: **Guy Comtois**. Sound: **Mark Ulano**. Music: **Charles Bernstein**. Costume designer: **Jack Buehler**. Make-up: **Robin Neal**. Special visual effects make-up: **Peter Knowlton**. Special-effects: **Rick Josephsen**. Animal action: **Karl Lewis Miller**. Colour: **CFI**.

RUNNING TIME:
**91 mins**

*Once upon a time, not so long ago, a monster came to the small town of Castle Rock, Maine.*

Please God
Get me
out of
here

**Cujo** (18)
*a new name for terror*

THE TAFT ENTERTAINMENT COMPANY Presents A DANIEL H. BLATT-ROBERT SINGER PRODUCTION DEE WALLACE in "CUJO" Starring DANIEL HUGH-KELLY DANNY PINTAURO ED LAUTER CHRISTOPHER STONE Music by CHARLES BERNSTEIN Based on the Novel by STEPHEN KING Screenplay by DON CARLOS DUNAWAY and LAUREN CURRIER Produced by DANIEL H. BLATT and ROBERT SINGER Directed by LEWIS TEAGUE

### SYNOPSIS

In a meadow not far from Castle Rock, Cujo, a loveable St Bernard, is bitten on the nose by a rabies-carrying bat. Within hours the disease has begun to affect him, and before the day is out he has killed his owner Joe Camber, who is a car mechanic, and Joe's long-time friend and neighbour, Gary Previer.

Back in town, the Trenton family is also having some problems. Little Tad is kept awake by his fear of 'monsters', while father Vic is about to leave town to deal with a business crisis when he learns that his wife, Donna, has been having an affair with a local carpenter, Steve Kemp.

Vic sets off, very distressed, leaving Donna to take her car to be fixed by Joe Camber. She and Tad drive out there, and only just reach Joe's yard before the car stalls. Cujo appears, with red eyes, matted fur and his face covered in foam. Tad goes into shock when Cujo attacks the car. During the next two days of blistering heat, Cujo continues to mount guard over the car, while Tad has frequent lapses into unconsciousness. A worried Vic returns to Castle Rock, and cannot understand what has happened to his family. Finally, Donna makes a break from the car. Cujo mauls her savagely, but she manages to kill him — at which point Vic arrives to find his wife and child only just alive.

'**Genuinely frightening** adaptation of Stephen King thriller about a woman and her son terrorized by rabid dog. Builds slowly but surely to terrifying (but not gory) climax. Not for children,' enthuses *Leonard Maltin's TV Movies and Video Guide.*

'A St Bernard dog is bitten by a rabies-infected bat and becomes a vicious killer. Not much of a basis for a horror film, and this is not much of a horror film,' is the dismissive verdict of *Halliwell's Film Guide.*

It would probably be fair to say that the vast majority of people who loved Stephen King's *The Shining* didn't like Stanley Kubrick's *THE SHINING* (1979), although some of them warmed to it later, after the initial shock had worn off. By contrast, fans of King's *Cujo* did like Lewis Teague's *CUJO*. Stephen King loved *CUJO.*

It would also be true to say that not many writers could successfully (in literary terms) keep a woman and child trapped in a car by a rabid dog for two-thirds of a thick book, and that not many directors would risk pinning themselves down to such a set-up for nearly half a movie.

■ Little Tad has seen something in his closet, something that was crouching low with huge bulking shoulders, glowing amber eyes and its face twisted into a snarl.

However, Stephen King and Lewis Teague were two such men and, fortunately, fate (in the guise of Taft Entertainment) brought them together.

There is, of course, more to the movie than Cujo and the car. There is, for instance, a little sub-plot surrounding surly mechanic Joe Camber. Mrs Camber — who is a woman about Donna Trenton's age, but has been life-worn to look a good 15 years older — has won a lottery. She buys Joe some garage equipment that he's been hungering after, in exchange for allowing her and son Brett to go away for a week to visit her sister. Her uncharismatic spouse nearly vetoes the plan — but then decides that he'll go up to Boston and 'have some fun'. He goes round to reveal his plans to boozing-mate Gary Previer and discovers the chewed-up mess that is all Cujo has left of him. Cujo is still there — and he savages Joe to death.

The episode at Gary Previer's is a very good audience warm-up for the long car-bound climax. Previer's reactions to Cujo establish how terrifying a proposition a rabid dog is, and the demolition of Previer's shack by Cujo, with just a few few 'lopes' and swipes of a paw, bring home just how huge Cujo is. It makes far more credible, in the final scenes, the idea that Cujo may well be able to crash his way into Donna's tightly-locked car.

Back in Castle Rock, the Trenton family have numerous issues to resolve. Vic, who is a partner in an advertising agency, is facing a nightmare at work. The breakfast cereal for which he has coined the brilliant slogan 'Nothing wrong here!' has caused whole families to end up in hospital with internal haemorrhaging. Vic is about to fly off to attempt to salvage the agency's reputation and thus avoid the possibility of bankruptcy, when he discovers that his family unit is equally unstable.

Next, there's Tad and his 'monsters'. Lewis Teague creates an unsettling moment when he opts for a toy-cupboard's eye view of frightened little Tad, suggesting a possible supernatural ingredient, but it never material-

■ Not a great day in the life of Donna Trenton. Her car battery is dead; the temperature in the car has risen to over 100 degrees; the water in the thermos is finished; little Tad is in a coma; a huge, mad dog won't let her get out of the car; and she hasn't got anything to read…

izes. Vic is very gentle with Tad, and writes down for him an anti-monster chant which they sing together at bedtime. Tad's reaction to rabid Cujo, before losing consciousness, is, 'Mummy, how did the monster get out of my cupboard?' At another shock-crazed moment Donna can just make out him whispering 'The Monster Words are no good.' As Vic sits in Donna's car at the end of the film, he sees a piece of paper under Tad's seat: it is the Monster Words.

Danny Pintauro makes a perfect Tad. He is heartbreakingly loveable

■ Tad finally goes into seizures, and Donna has to leave the car with him and make a run for Camber house. Even after she shoots Cujo, the power of madness enables the dog to send her sprawling.

## KING ON CUJO

*'It's one of the scariest things I've ever seen. It's terrifying! I think this guy [Lewis Teague] is the most unsung film director in America. He has absolutely no shame and no moral sense. He just wants to go get ya, and I relate to that!'*

*'CUJO is my favourite adaptation [of the films made by that date] because it's big and bad and not very bright ... it just stands in one place and keeps punching away.'*

and vulnerable; and if a horror-film director can get you to care about his characters — he's got you. Dee Wallace wins her audience round to Donna by the end, too. She had quite a hard task. Donna doesn't start out as too endearing. She is so bored with her handsome, successful, loving husband (and Tad's very caring father), her adorable son and her lovely house that she takes up with the local heart-throb — who clearly does not have any depth. Ironically, she is just telling Steve that their affair is over when Vic comes in unexpectedly.

However, she does have to carry the shroud of guilt with her for the rest of the film: obviously what happens to her and Tad is 'all her fault'. But her concern for her child is so absolute, and her situation in the car so pitiful, that she has earned the viewers' forgiveness by the end. She clearly earns the director's forgiveness too, in that she's permitted to survive the severe bites of a rabid dog.

Cujo just about manages to overcome the biggest problem of his role — which is that (being a cuddly St Bernards) he was grossly miscast. It is irrelevant that 'Cujo' is a South American word that translates as 'unconquerable force'.

It doesn't matter how much foam and 'blood' and goo has been plastered onto him, or how expertly he's been persuaded to look fierce, it is nevertheless almost impossible to turn a St Bernard into anything other than a large, loveable pooch. It is a testimony to the acting, direction and camerawork that movie-watchers were able to surmount this hurdle and find themselves chilled to the core by Cujo's vicious vigil.

Stephen King claims that he wrote *Cujo* when his mother, perturbed by his endless stream of macabre tales, said, 'Why don't you write a nice story about a faithful dog?' King obliged, but, he ruefully points out, 'the dog turned out to be rabid and ate a whole lot of folks up.'

■ Cujo, 200 pounds of horrible hound, trying to claw his way into the Trentons' Pinto. He's lost all lovability by this time, and poses a serious danger to the St. Bernard market.

## IT WAS THE DOG THAT DIED

*In the novel, Tad dies. It has always been a troubling issue for King: 'In the novel, but not in the film, the kid died and I got a lot of letters from people who said, "How could you let that happen?" King's response was that sometimes children do die … 'And the only thing I could write back is, "I'm not God. I just wrote the damned book. He died. I didn't want him to die."'*

(From an interview with Stephen King, by Matt Schaffer, on WBCN-FM Radio-s, October 1983.)

*When King gave the book to his publisher, his editor had said, 'What would you think of the kid living?' King replied, 'That's not negotiable; the kid died.' His view of films, however, is that they're not life … 'Films exist on a much more emotional level. It's all happening in front of you. So when Taft brought this up again, I said, "Fine, let the kid live and see how that works."'*

(From an interview with Stephen King in Cinefantastique magazine, December 1983.)

## The Films of Stephen King

# The Dead Zone

## 1983

*Awake in the dead zone and awake .... into a nightmare*

DIRECTOR:
**David Cronenberg**
*(USA, 1983)*

LEADING PLAYERS:
**Christopher Walken**
(Johnny Smith), **Brooke
Adams** (Sarah Bracknell),
**Tom Skerritt** (Sheriff
Bannerman), **Herbert Lom**
(Dr Sam Weizak), **Anthony
Zerbe** (Roger Stuart),
**Colleen Dewhurst**
(Henrietta Dodd), **Martin
Sheen** (Greg Stillson),
**Nicholas Campbell** (Frank
Dodd), **Sean Sullivan** (Herb
Smith), **Jackie Burroughs**
(Vera Smith), **Geza Kovacs**
(Sonny Elliman), **Roberta
Weiss**, (Alma Frechette),
**Simon Craig** (Chris Stuart),
**Peter Dvorsky** (Dardis),
**Julie-Ann Heathwood**
(Amy), **Barry Flatman** (Walt).

PRODUCTION COMPANY:
**Dino De Laurentiis
Corporation**

PRODUCER:
**Debra Hill**

SCREENPLAY:
**Jeffrey Boam**, based on the
novel by **Stephen King**.

Photographer: **Mark Irwin**.
Editor: **Ronald Sanders**.
Production designer: **Carol
Spier**. Art director: **Barbara
Dunphy**. Sound: **Brian Day**.
Music: **Michael Kamen**.
Costume design: **Olga
Dimitrov**. Make-up:
**Shonagh Jabour**. Special-
effects co-ordinator: **John
Belyeu**. Stunt
co-ordinators: **Dick
Warlock, Carey Loftin**.
Technicolor. Dolby stereo.

RUNNING TIME:
**103 mins**

### SYNOPSIS

A car crash leaves schoolteacher Johnny Smith in a coma. He awakens in a hospital to discover that he has lost five years of his life, and that his girlfriend, Sarah, is now married and has a son called Denny. Johnny has, however, gained a 'gift' (or a curse): when he touches someone he can 'see' into their past, present and future. His first 'vision' enables him to warn his nurse that her daughter is trapped in a fire. Thereafter he 'sees' that the mother of his sympathetic physician, Dr Weizak, did not, as the doctor had always believed, die in the holocaust.

News of Johnny's 'gift' spreads. He is inundated with people needing help. Even the local Sheriff seeks his aid in solving a series of gruesome murders. Johnny has to get away, for the use of his 'gift' is also draining his life-force away, and so he disappears to a far-off town. There, he comes to realize that he cannot deny his power and the responsibilities it carries.

He returns to his home town of Castle Rock and meets Greg Stillson, a charming, man-of-the-people politician whose campaign Sarah is supporting. But on shaking his hand, Johnny 'sees' Stillson becoming President of the USA and pressing the fatal nuclear button. Johnny decides that he must stop Stillson; he attempts to shoot him at a political rally but misses and is himself fatally wounded. However, at the sound of the shot, Stillson grabs little Denny as a shield. Johnny's last vision is of Stillson committing suicide after a photograph of his cowardice is published.

In his mind,
he has the power
to see the future.
In his hands,
he has the power
to change it.

Stephen King's

*THE DEAD ZONE* took a while to get into production. After the novel was published in 1979 and hit the best-seller lists, movie rights were acquired by Lorimar, who hired screenwriter Jeffrey Boam to start on the screenplay. A Lorimar executive then approached David Cronenberg as director — only to retract apologetically on learning that another executive had just signed up Stanley Donen as director and Sydney Pollack as producer. However, the company shortly thereafter fell into hard times, and subsequently liquidated its feature-film department.

Next, *THE DEAD ZONE*'s movie rights passed into the hands of movie mogul Dino De Laurentiis. He appointed Debra Hill (of *HALLOWEEN*'s *1*, *2* and *3*) producer, and the person she favoured as director, having greatly admired his then recently released *VIDEODROME*, was — David Cronenberg.

Cronenberg had, by this time, a healthy reputation for 'unhealthy' films including: *SHIVERS* (1975) — bizarre, sexually oriented parasites run rampant through occupants of high-rise buildings; *SCANNERS* (1981) — a group of telepathic social misfits who plug into people's nervous systems and blow their heads apart; and *VIDEODROME* (1983) — a video TV programmer discovers how to beam his hard-core movies into his viewers,

dreams. If he'd just dream a little more normally, I'd love to work with him again.'

Cronenberg and King seemed in many ways made for each other. But for both of them this was a step out of line. King's book wasn't the usual King-type horror; and Cronenberg had never before worked from anyone else's story. Nevertheless, both looked forward to this original experience.

There still remained the little matter of a shooting script. De Laurentiis hadn't liked Jeffrey Boam's first version, and asked Stephen King to do one. He didn't like that either, finding it, as King remembers 'too involved', too convoluted'. In the end, Cronenberg, Boam and Hill secluded

■ Shortly after emerging from his long coma, Johnny is catapulted into the first of his psychic visions. This one is hot stuff, the burning bedroom of his nurse's little girl.

and not just their sets. 'Outlandish', 'bizarre', 'brilliant', 'tasteless', 'stunning' were all equally likely to be applied to his films. He certainly had become a cult favourite, and was dubbed 'The Prince of Blood', but few dismissed his creative talents: it was what he did with them that didn't always go down too well. James Wood, the star of *VIDEODROME* commented: 'He works from his

themselves away to work on it until they felt they'd got it right.

Mark Irwin, director of photography, and Carol Spier, production designer, designed the 'New England' sets and locations as if they had been painted by Norman Rockwell, the prolific post-war illustrator whose work was noted for his idyllic view of middle-Americana. The Canadian town of Niagara-on-the-Lake was chosen as the stand-in for 'Castle Rock', Maine. There, cast and crew had to contend with the coldest winter temperatures for 30 years. Still, it did help with providing the bleak, white landscapes which echoed the wintry tone of this tale. The Big Freeze was, however, rapidly followed by the warmest winter weather in over 140 years, necessitating great quantities of 'cotton wool'.

Toronto's Lakeshore Studios were the setting for the special-effects shots, the most elaborate of which was the little girl's blazing bedroom,

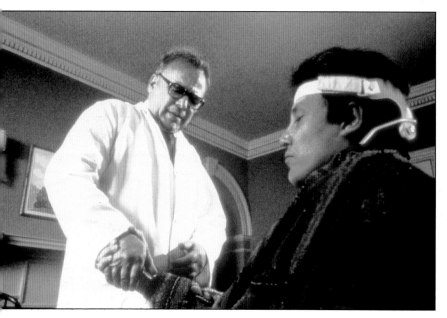

■ Johnny's second psychic 'flash', on taking Dr Weizak's hand, hurtles him into war-torn Europe, where he sees Weizak's mother throw her little son into a cart filled with Jews fleeing from the Nazis.

Johnny's first vision on awakening from his five-year trance. Special-effects co-ordinator Jon Belyeu and stunt co-ordinator Dick Warlock designed a re-shootable set, one which could be restored to its pre-conflagration state, complete with new wallpaper, in less time than it took to have a tea-break.

The most gory and 'Cronenberg' of the effects was the suicide of Deputy Frank Dodd, when he was about to be apprehended for the Castle Rock murders. He used scissors .... Blood? They must have used up all the ketchup in Ontario.

Christopher Walken and Martin Sheen were beautifully matched as the symbols of Good and Evil; as the True Seer and the False Seer. Walken's pale, enigmatic face is magnetically unfathomable, and rivets attention even when, for much of the film, his character is gently passive or bravely lonely — neither of which are show-stopping attributes. Sheen, as Greg Stillson, is the False Seer, the energetic charismatic who sweeps people before him to form the red carpet up the stairway to his ill-gotten success. Johnny's is a bleeding heart; Stillson hasn't got one.

Walken's Johnny is a man who has been marked out, and thus isolated,

## CHANGING THE ZONE

Stephen King's novel intertwines, from the outset, the stories of Johnny Smith and Greg Stillson. We learn that Johnny's 'gift' had already been triggered as a kid, and that Stillson had had a dreadful childhood, beaten and otherwise abused. Cronenberg did shoot an episode of Johnny's childhood, but later abandoned it, focussing on Johnny as an adult, and also bringing in Stillson fully grown and fully warped. In the novel, *The Dead Zone* is a blank area in Johnny's 'seeing', one where the future could not be foretold; and the book's end reveals that this was caused by a brain tumour that Johnny has had all along.

In the movie, Johnny experiences his visions, he is 'in' them, and the pain and helplessness of witnessing the crimes of Deputy Frank Dodd and Greg Stillson motivate his decision to stop Stillson at any price. In the book, the child Stillson uses to shield himself with is randomly grabbed from the crowd; in the movie, it becomes Sarah's child — a script change brought about by a chance remark from Christopher Walken. How did Stephen King feel about the changes? According to Cronenberg: 'He said that there are some things in the movie which he wished he'd done in the book — which I thought was high praise.'

by fate (a theme common to both King's and Cronenberg's work). Whenever he touches someone's hand, he gets a visual 'newsflash' of some incident or important time in their lives. His road is hard, and he starts to avoid touching people. But he comes to accept that he has to do whatever this 'gift' enables him to do.

At the same time, his powers are disempowering him and causing him to waste away. Each time he 'sees', he ages greatly and comes closer to death; each 'seeing' is a trip into *THE DEAD ZONE*.

## KING ON THE DEAD ZONE

'Cronenberg did one of the great jobs of his life. It's still one of the great directorial turnarounds, away from all this sort of cold, polished, high-tech stuff that he'd done before and after. He just opted for this sort of folksy New Hampshire. He got tremendous performances out of people....'

'THE DEAD ZONE.... had a lot of incidents, it covered a long period of time, the characters went through a number of changes, and a lot of that necessarily had to be chopped and channelled for the movie so that they kept the main relationships .... it was a rich movie ... but it didn't have the richness of incident and the wealth of characters that the book had.

(From an interview with Stephen King, published in Cinefantastique magazine, February 1991.)

■ *Above*: Johnny finds himself 'watching' a girl being murdered by none other than Deputy Sheriff Frank Dodd.
■ *Below*: On shaking the hand of political candidate Greg Stillson, Johnny sees his ruthless intentions.

# Christine 1983

DIRECTOR:
**John Carpenter**
*(USA, 1983)*

LEADING PLAYERS:
**Keith Gordon** (Arnie Cunningham), **John Stockwell** (Dennis Guilder), **Alexandra Paul** (Leigh Cabot), **Robert Prosky** (Will Darnell), **Harry Dean Stanton** (Rudolph Junkins), **Christine Belford** (Regina Cunningham), **Roberts Blossom** (George LeBay), **William Ostrander** (Buddy), **David Spielberg** (Mr Casey), **Malcolm Danare** (Moochie), **Steven Tash** (Rich), **Stuart Charno** (Vanderberg), **Kelly Preston** (Roseanne), **Marc Poppel** (Chuck), **Robert Darnell** (Michael Cunningham).

PRODUCTION COMPANY:
**Columbia Picture Industries-Delphi/Richard Kobritz**

PRODUCER:
**Richard Kobritz**

CO-PRODUCER:
**Larry Franco**

SCREENPLAY:
**Bill Phillips**: based on the novel by **Stephen King**.

Photography: **Donald M. Morgan**. Editor: **Marion Rothman**. Production designer: **Daniel Lomino**. Sound: **Thomas Causey**. Music: **John Carpenter**, in association with **Alan Howarth**. Costume design (women's): **Dawn Jackson**. Make-up: **Bob Dawn**. Special-effects supervisor: **Roy Arbogast**. Stunt co-ordinator: **Terry Leonard**. Colour: **Technicolor**; prints by **Metrocolor**. Panavision. Dolby stereo.

RUNNING TIME:
**110 mins**

*What if a car were born to be bad? What if it had a mind of its own?*

## SYNOPSIS

On a car assembly line, a shiny red-and-white 1958 Plymouth Fury is proving a menace. Before she leaves the Chrysler factory she has killed one man and dismembered another. Twenty years later, Dennis Guilder, a high-school football captain, is out driving with his friend Arnie Cunningham, the high-school misfit, when they pass the same '58 Fury, now a rusting wreck. Arnie buys the car (named Christine by its former owner), despite Dennis's misgivings. He takes her off to a garage, and, in an astonishingly short time, Christine is transformed into her gleaming former self. Arnie changes too; becoming first very 'cool' and then quite ruthless. Leigh, the school's attractive new girl, falls for Arnie and gets more and more jealous of his passion for Christine — who retaliates by trapping Leigh inside her locked doors and windows, whereupon the girl very nearly chokes to death.

When a gang of envious classmates reduce Christine to a pile of scrap, she miraculously repairs herself, sets off in pursuit of the creeps, and demolishes each in turn. Leigh and Dennis decide that Arnie must be saved from his murderous car. They corner her in a garage, and crush her with a steamroller — discovering, too late, that Arnie is in the driving seat. Later, at the scrapyard, Leigh and Dennis look at the lump of metal which was Christine, but don't notice that a bit of it has begun to unravel ...

**S**tephen King's *Christine* was at the top of the best-seller lists when John Carpenter began shooting his *CHRISTINE*. The novel's potential had been spotted when it was still in manuscript form by Richard Kobritz, the film's producer, who felt that it was a winning combination of teenagers, rock music and automobiles. Kobritz had worked with John Carpenter before, and felt he would be the right director. Carpenter already had a number of successful thrillers and horrors under his belt, including *ASSAULT ON PRECINCT 13* (1976), *SOMEONE'S WATCHING ME* (TV, 1977), *HALLOWEEN* (1978), *THE FOG* (1979) and *THE THING* (1982). Kobritz also knew that Carpenter was available because his production of *FIRESTARTER* had just folded, having proven too expensive.

Kobritz, Carpenter and scriptwriter Bill Phillips were all agreed that Christine was the star of the show and mustn't be upstaged. They therefore

■ Leigh has the nerve to suggest that Christine might be taking up too much of Arnie's time. Christine overhears, and before you could say 'Coming right up', Leigh all but terminally chokes on her burger.

hired relative unknowns for the young leads — Arnie, Dennis and Leigh — although Keith Gordon had been acclaimed in Brian De Palma's *DRESSED TO KILL* (1980). The acting 'muscle' went into the character roles: Harry Dean Stanton as Police Detective Junkins (who, unfortunately, wasn't given much to do); Roberts Blossom as LeBay, Christine's hoary, bleary-eyed former owner; and Robert Prosky (who stole all his scenes) as Will

## QUEEN OF THE ROAD

Christine is a classic *femme fatale*: elegant, sexy, irresistible, temperamental, calculating, more or less heartless and, when necessary, lethal.

Casting for the role of Christine got under way. Ads were placed in big cities, a hotline was set up to car scrapyards, and the Department of Motor Vehicles in California helped contact owners of '58 Plymouth Furies. In the end, dozens were bought or borrowed, and as many as 14 of them — in different stages of rust or polish — were at work on the set at any one time.

Roy Arbogast, special-effects expert, was responsible for coaching Christine into her starring role. It was thanks to Arbogast's training that, after scenes in which she'd been all but demolished, Christine learned how to pop her headlights back into place, uncrimp her hood, straighten out her wings — and blaze back to life

again. Arbogast made model sections of Christine out of moulded polyurethane. By tightening straps attached to the back of various sections, he could produce dents which would miraculously straighten out on being released. However, many of Christine's more spectacular recoveries were the result of running the film of her demolition in reverse.

Christine clearly established herself as a living, breathing character, even with cast and crew, who never referred to her as 'the car' or 'the Plymouth' or 'it'. She was always 'her'; always 'Christine'.

■ Arnie (below) with doubtful friend Dennis, about to buy a beaten-up Christine from George Le Bay. Soon, Arnie will have restored her to her previous splendour.

## KING ON CHRISTINE

*'I thought CHRISTINE would be a hit. It seemed such a natural. And I wasn't the only one, you know. The people at Columbia obviously felt that way ... They rushed it into production. It seemed like it just should be there, and it just wasn't.*

*'I went to CHRISTINE with Kirby McCauley, my agent. People just sat there. Nobody cat-called or laughed. And nobody was getting into it either. It was like this dead engine. Every now and then it would cough and sputter a bit.*

*'There is some of the excitement that he [Carpenter] can generate. When the car's going along the road and it's chasing these people, that's pretty good.'*

(From an interview by Gary Wood, in Cinefantastique magazine, Feb 1991.)

Darnell, owner of the repair shop where Christine becomes transformed from the worn, rusty heap bought by Arnie into gleaming evil.

The lyrics of 1950s pop songs were used extensively by King in his novel. In the film, they become Christine's language. Her radio only plays 1950s numbers, and the songs that blare forth from her dashboard give a clear indication of her mood. She emerges from the assembly line warning the world that she's 'Bad to the Bone', and tells Arnie that she's 'Pledging My Love' and that 'We Belong Together'. She can be blackly humorous, too: when she has locked her doors so Arnie can't get in to rescue asphyxiating Leigh, she pounds out 'Keep A-Knockin' But You Can't Come In'.

In the novel, Christine's former owner, LeBay, is a demonically possessed man whose spirit lives on in the car and takes possession of Arnie. Some critics of *CHRISTINE* felt that, in trying to transfer the wickedness to Christine herself, some crucial horror element got lost. Carpenter agreed. 'It wasn't scary,' he said later. 'I made a big mistake by taking out Roland LeBay's rotting corpse in the back seat. I guess I was just tired of rotting corpses at the time, and tried to do it all with the car. I failed.'

Many disagreed, finding in the film both King's and Carpenter's strengths mingling and sparking well. There was even a tease in the ending, leaving the door open for Christine to rise and roar across the screen again — 'But She Ain't Done Nothin' Yet'.

■ Leigh and Dennis decide that Christine is too possessive, too vengeful and too dangerous, and that she has to go. They lure her to a garage, and crush her with a caterpillar truck. Unfortunately, they forget to remove Arnie first.

# Children of the Corn

## 1984

*In the cornfield there were no bugs, no crows, no weeds, no wind. Yet the corn was rustling. How could that be?*

**DIRECTOR:**
**Fritz Kiersch**
*(USA, 1984)*

**LEADING PLAYERS:**
**Peter Horton** (Dr Burt Stanton), **Linda Hamilton** (Vicky Baxter), **R.G. Armstrong** (Chest Diehl), **John Franklin** (Isaac), **Courtney Gains** (Malachai), **Robby Kiger** (Job), **Anne-Marie McEvoy** (Sarah), **Julie Maddalena** (Rachel), **Jonas Marlowe** (Joseph), **John Philbin** (Amos).

**PRODUCTION COMPANY:**
**New World Pictures/Angeles Entertainment Group/ Cinema Group Ventures.**

**PRODUCERS:**
**Donald P. Borchers, Terrence Kirby**

**SCREENPLAY:**
**George Goldsmith**; based on the short story by **Stephen King**.

Photographer: **Raoul Lomas**. Editor: **Harry Keramidas**. Art director: **Craig Stearns**. Sound: **Jon 'Earl' Stein**. Music: **Jonathan Elias**. Costume designer: **Barbara Scott**. Make-up: **Erica Ueland**. Special visual effects: **Max W. Anderson**. Colour: **CFI**.

**RUNNING TIME:**
**93 mins**

## SYNOPSIS

Dr Burt Stanton is travelling through Nebraska with his girlfriend, Vicky Baxter, on his way to Seattle. While driving through the cornfields they run over a boy, but Burt finds that his throat has already been cut. The couple drive on into nearby Gatlin which, they discover, is inhabited by children who have murdered their parents. The children belong to a religious cult, led by Isaac, which worships a mysterious evil Being called 'He Who Walks Behind the Rows'.

The children themselves are destined to die in sacrifice to the blood-hungry deity on their 19th birthdays. However, they are short of 'offerings' at this time and so they kidnap Vicky. Two children, Sarah and Job, who are not cult members, help Burt to look for her. Malachai, the cult's second-in-command, then stages a revolt against Isaac and kills him; but Isaac returns from the dead, seeking revenge. The Corn Demon himself also appears, threatening to destroy everyone. Burt, with Job's help, averts disaster by setting fire to the cornfields. He convinces the children that 'He Who Walks Behind the Rows' has never been a fit subject for worship. Burt, Vicky, Job and Sarah then drive away.

The main difficulty in filming *CHILDREN OF THE CORN* was the corn. The idea of making a film from this Stephen King short story had been around for several years. King himself had done a screenplay (although when the film did come to be made, it wasn't used). At one point, Roger Corman's New World company seemed interested, but later decided against it. However, after Corman sold New World, its new owners decided to

■ Isaac, a sinister child who serves the Demon God of the cornfields, determines the fate of all who mistakenly stumble into the little town of Gatlin.

revive the idea and approached Fritz Kiersch, who was then busy directing commercials. Kiersch remembers that he was given the job at the beginning of August, and that two days later he was flying to Iowa to find locations. After three weeks of pre-production, filming commenced.

The reason for all the haste was — the corn. It was nearly ripe. Another few weeks and it would be gone. All the cornfield shots, and all corn-connected special effects, had to be the ones to be filmed first.

The second difficulty was 'He Who Walks Behind the Rows'. New World executives harangued Kiersch daily as to what it was going to look like. Kiersch and George Goldsmith, the scriptwriter, were agreed that a horror-type monster, however well done, could create an irretrievable anti-climax. They decided that they would put the bulk of their (very small) budget into showing the trail of destruction and terror that the Guardian of the Blood-hungry Corn leaves behind him. 'He has the ability

## SECOND DEADLY HARVEST

*CHILDREN OF THE CORN II: THE FINAL SACRIFICE* (1993) was the second of the King sequels. It took its premise from King's original story, but had no other input by him. This time directed by David F. Brice, the film opens with a quick synopsis of 'Evil Corn Dolly I', and then carries straight on.

After three years, the neighbours finally notice that something is amiss when they unearth the bodies of the townsfolk of Gatlin in a corn-field. John Garrett, a journalist, and son Danny become involved when John goes to Gatlin in the hope of getting a page-one story that will boost his flagging career.

The neighbouring town of Hemingford adopts the remaining Gatlin children — including Micah,

who quickly re-forms the 'He Who Walks Behind the Rows' cult: it seems the great Bogey of the Cornfields was not destroyed after all. This time, some adults are murdered by the kids, and some by unexplained supernatural forces: in one of the film's best scenes a man dies in church from a killer nosebleed.

This time there's a sub-plot. The good people of Hemingford are resisting enquiries into the Gatlin atrocities because they want to boost their corn yield by mixing it with inedible corn that's been infected with a deadly form of mould.

Could it be, we are left wondering, that terminal nosebleeds, murder-ous children and a deadly Corn Spirit are the result of aflotoxins? A terrifying climax is but a gasp away.

■ Murderous Malachai leads a successful revolt against Isaac's rule over the corn kiddies.

■ Two of the children appear to have been completely unaffected by the murder and mayhem that has gone on around them. One of them, Job, helps Dr Burt Stanton to escape.

to make the earth move, the clouds come in, the corn part,' said Goldsmith. 'That's where most of the special effects come in. You see the capabilities but not the monster.'

The end of the film departed radically from King's book in which both Vicky and Burt are caught by the children and 'sacrificed', and 'He Who Walks ....' lives on contentedly. As with *CUJO* (1983), anxieties about how this would affect the box-office won out, and Vicky and Burt were preserved. However, box-office considerations seemed to have less prudently governed the film's opening scenes, during which the children of Gatlin brutally murder their parents in a number of inventive ways. There was no way of empathising with the kids after that — except for two strange little misfits: Job and Sarah.

Job's witnessing of the butchery of his father had not won him over to Isaac, but neither did it leave him murderously inclined or psychologically wrecked. Job appears to be a perfectly 'normal' little boy. However, we have no suspenseful anxieties over Job's safety because we know he survives. Why? His voice narrates the story. His sister Sarah is psychic. She 'knows' when someone is on their way

## KING ON CHILDREN OF THE CORN

'My feeling ... [for most movies made from his books] is like a guy who sends his daughter off to college. You hope she'll do well. You hope she won't fall in with the wrong people. You hope she won't be raped at a fraternity party, which is pretty well what happened to CHILDREN OF THE CORN ...'

*(From an interview with Stephen King, by Craig Modderno, published in USA Today, May 1985.)*

to Gatlin, and can draw their portrait. An invaluable asset, one would think, but the children have found no role for Sarah's gifts. Why not?

*CHILDREN OF THE CORN* is, in fact, a 'how long is a piece of string?' movie. What is 'He Who Walks Behind the Rows'? How has Isaac persuaded everyone to follow his preaching? What happened to the dead kid Vicky and Burt picked up off the road? Having encountered the murderous religious community, why does Burt trust Job and Sarah? Why don't Burt and Vicky high-tail it out of there? How come the absence of the entire adult population of Gatlin has gone unnoticed in the outside world for more than three years?

For those wishing answers to those questions, *CHILDREN OF THE CORN* is the wrong film. If you can suspend disbelief — it's a treasure trove.

# Firestarter 1984

DIRECTOR:
**Mark L. Lester**
*(USA, 1984)*

LEADING PLAYERS:
**David Keith** (Andrew McGee), **Drew Barrymore** (Charlie McGee), **Freddie Jones** (Dr Joseph Wanless), **Heather Locklear** (Vicky McGee), **Martin Sheen** (Captain Hollister), **George C. Scott** (John Rainbird), **Art Carney** (Irv Manders), **Louise Fletcher** (Norma Manders), **Moses Gunn** (Dr Pynchot), **Antonio Fargas** (taxi driver), **Drew Snyder** (Orville Jamieson), **Curtis Credel** (Bates), **Keith Colbert** (Mayo), **Richard Warlock** (Knowles), **Jeff Ramsey** (Steinowitz), **Stanley Mann** (motel owner).

PRODUCTION COMPANY:
**Universal Pictures**

PRODUCER:
**Frank Capra Jnr**

SCREENPLAY:
**Stanley Mann**: based on the novel by **Stephen King**

Photographer: **Giuseppe Ruzzolini**. Editor: **David Rawlins**. Art director: **Giorgio Postiglione**. Sound: **David Hildyard**. Music: **Tangerine Dream**. Costumers: **Wes Eckhardt, Jennifer Butler**. Make-up effects: **Jos Antonio Sanchez**, (George C. Scott) **Del Acevedo**. Special effects: **Mike Wood, Jeff Jarvis**. Stunt co-ordinator: **Glenn Randall Jnr**. **Technicolor**.

RUNNING TIME:
**115 mins.**

*'Burn it down, Charlie. Burn it all down!'*

Charlie McGee is Stephen King's

FIRESTARTER

Charlie McGee is a happy, healthy eight-year-old little girl. Normal in every way but one.

She has the power to set objects afire with just one glance.

It's a power she does not want. It's a power she cannot control. And, each night, Charlie prays to be just like every other child.

But there are those who will do everything in their power to find her, control her... or destroy her.

DINO DE LAURENTIIS presents "FIRESTARTER" DAVID KEITH · DREW BARRYMORE · FREDDIE JONES HEATHER LOCKLEAR · MARTIN SHEEN · GEORGE C. SCOTT · ART CARNEY · LOUISE FLETCHER Screenplay by STANLEY MANN Based on the novel by STEPHEN KING Music by TANGERINE DREAM Associate Producer MARTHA SCHUMACHER Produced by FRANK CAPRA Jr. Directed by MARK L. LESTER A UNIVERSAL RELEASE DISTRIBUTED BY UIP READ THE FUTURA PAPERBACK SOUNDTRACK AVAILABLE ON MCA RECORDS AND CASSETTES

## SYNOPSIS

When they were impoverished students, Andy and Vicky took part in experiments being run by 'The Shop', a government-run outfit engaged in extremely dubious and dangerous scientific research. The mind-bending drugs they were given left Andy with psychic powers that enable him to control the actions of others; and their child, Charlie, is born pyrokinetic — a 'fireraiser'.

The Shop now wants Charlie back, and kidnaps her, killing her mother in the process. Andy uses his own, now-waning, powers to rescue Charlie, but from then on they are on the run. At The Shop's headquarters, project leader Captain Hollister details professional assassin John Rainbird to find Charlie. Andy and Charlie are in hiding with a kindly farmer and his wife, Irv and Norma Manders. When Shop agents find them there, Charlie exterminates them but she is so appalled by her actions that she vows not to kill again.

Rainbird recaptures Andy and Charlie by shooting them with drugged darts. He tells Charlie she can see her father if she cooperates with The Shop's experiments. Andy psychically 'pushes' Hollister to help him and Charlie escape. Rainbird gives chase and shoots Hollister and Andy. As he dies, Andy tells Charlie to break her vow and burn down The Shop and those working for it. She does so and then returns to Norma and Irv, who take her to tell her story to the national newspapers.

**FIRESTARTER** had a quite extraordinary number of things operating in its favour, including its source material, its script, its stars and its special effects. However, when it came to turning these promising ingredients into a zippy little thriller, the general feeling was that someone forgot to put in the zip.

First of the plus factors was that it was based on a bestselling novel by Stephen King. Secondly, it was *closely* based on King's novel: Stanley Mann's adaptation was 'a masterpiece', affirmed King. Then, it had a

phenomenal cast. Drew Barrymore was a pre-teeny starlet after her role in *E.T.* (1982); David Keith had moved into the limelight with *AN OFFICER AND A GENTLEMAN* (1981); George C. Scott already had four Oscar-nominations and had won one for *PATTON* (1969); Martin Sheen had an Emmy Award behind him, a fine collection of excellent TV-movie performances, and had been acclaimed for his role of two-faced politico Greg Stillson in *THE DEAD ZONE*. Art Carney had become a leading character actor following his Oscar for his first starring role in *HARRY AND TONTO* (1974); Louise Fletcher won her Oscar for *ONE FLEW OVER THE CUCKOO'S NEST* (1975). In addition there was the renowned British Shakespearean actor Freddie Jones; powerful American lead Moses Gunn; and one of the stars of TV's *DYNASTY*, Heather Locklear.

*FIRESTARTER* provided, on top of all that star-power, a phenomenal feast of pyrotechnic effects and stunts. There were trenches of fire, flying fireballs, walls of flame, multiple car explosions and the destruction of a full-scale replica of an old Southern plantation. A whole team of stunt-persons were repeatedly engulfed in flames before being catapulted into the air or tossed out of windows.

Stephen King had reservations about both the casting and the effects. 'The movie had great actors,' he said, 'with the exception of David Keith, who I didn't feel was very good ... Martin Sheen, who is a great actor ... [had] nobody to pull him in ... he simply reprised Greg Stillson [from *The Dead Zone*]. That's all there is; it's the same character exactly. But Greg Stillson should not be in charge of The Shop. He's not the kind of guy who gets that job.' King also thought that Art Carney's role didn't work, and that George C. Scott — a 'brilliant' actor — came over as 'stiff'.

As regards the spectacle, King said, 'There are things that happen in terms of special effects in that movie that make no sense to me whatsoever. Why this kid's [Drew Barrymore's] hair blows every time she starts fires is totally beyond my understanding.' King was also strongly of the opinion that production-chief Dino De Laurentiis's passion for the spectacular (De Laurentiis had been the force behind such epic fantasies as *ULYSSES* (1955), *BARABBAS* (1962), and *BARBARELLA* (1968), more than likely impeded the vision of the entire film-making crew.

One way or another, Stephen King and director Mark Lester were in marked disagreement over the film's outcome. Lester insisted that: 'During the course of filming he [King] visited the set, watched the dailies, and was extremely excited about the movie .... After the movie came out, I was appalled at some of the things he said.' King remembers differently: 'I only met him [Mark] twice, and very briefly.... Mark's assertion that I saw the movie and loved it is erroneous. I saw *part* of an early rough cut. When I saw the final cut, months later ... I

■ John Rainbird, The Shop's most cunning operative, has an interest in Charlie that is more than just professional. He believes that, if he can get her to confide in him, he can steal her powers.

was extremely depressed. The parts were all there, but the total was somehow less than the parts ....'

The problem seems to have been that everyone tried too hard to be faithful to King. Mann stuck closely to the book, but the book — like many of King's works — was far harder to translate into cinema than it seemed. Both director and scriptwriter appear to have been worshipfully respectful of the novel (except for a few lines — and the aforementioned effects — to which King took exception). Sadly, instead of this producing quintessential King, the reverse happened. The film seemed static, wooden, careful, and all traces of 'King' had vanished.

■ Andy's own psychic powers are fading fast. To protect his daughter from The Shop's unscrupulous operatives, he must rely on his wits and courage, and they are no match for Rainbird's drugged darts.

## KING ON FIRESTARTER

*'Firestarter is one of the worst of the bunch [of movies that have been made of my work] .... it's flavourless; it's like cafeteria mashed potatoes.'*

*'There were $3 million worth of special effects and another $3 million worth of Academy Award-winning talent up there on the screen, and none of it was working. Watching that happen was an incredible, unreal, and painful experience.'*

*(From an interview with Stephen King, published in* American Film *magazine, June 1986.)*

# Cat's Eye 1985

*Nine lives ain't much when you're having to walk on the wild side*

## SYNOPSIS

This film is based on two of King's short stories, 'Quitter Inc.' and 'The Ledge' and includes another storyline, 'The General', written by King just for the film.

*THE STORY-OPENER*: A cat in Wilmington, N. Carolina, sees in a store window the 'vision' of a little girl begging for its help. Before the cat can find her, it is diverted by a couple of misadventures:

*QUITTERS, INC.*: In New York the cat is picked up by 'Dr' Donatti, who is using his 'hair-raising' aversion-therapy techniques to ensure that Morrison, who desperately wants to stop smoking, kicks the habit. When Morrison decides he can safely cheat in a thick traffic-jam, his punishment is to watch his wife suffer a series of electric shocks.

*THE LEDGE*: In Atlantic City, Cressner, a compulsive gambler, sees the cat trying to cross a busy road and bets his companions that the cat will make it. When it does, Cressner takes it back to his skyscraper penthouse where he has a revenge planned for Norris, his wife's lover: Norris must walk along a narrow ledge around the top of the apartment building, or be framed for a drugs deal. Norris succeeds — and then turns the tables on Cressner, who falls to his death.

*THE GENERAL*: In Wilmington, N. Carolina, the cat is found and adopted by the little girl it is looking for; she christens it 'The General'. Sally Ann, the girl's mother, is superstitious of cats, believing they can kill a sleeping child by stealing its breath away, but in fact the threat lies in a tiny, evil Troll who lives behind the skirting board. The Troll is vicious and cunning, but eventually the cat succeeds in its mission to slay the monster and rescue the child.

While *FIRESTARTER* (1984) was in progress, movie mogul Dino De Laurentiis found himself very impressed with its child star, little Drew Barrymore. He asked Stephen King if he would write another script for Drew. Not only that, De Laurentiis had acquired (from English producer Milton Subotsky) King's stories 'Quitters Inc.' and 'The Ledge', and he wanted King to adapt these for the screen — and link them to his 'Drew' screenplay. King has described how hard he finds it to say 'no' to De

DIRECTOR:
**Lewis Teague**
*(USA, 1985)*

LEADING PLAYERS:
*QUITTERS, INC.:*
**James Woods** (Morrison), **Alan King** (Donatti), **Tony Munafo** (Junk), **Mary D'Arcy** (Cindy), **Russell Horton** (Milquetoast), **Patricia Benson** (Mrs Milquetoast).
*THE LEDGE:*
**Robert Hays** (Norris), **Kenneth McMillan** (Cressner), **Jess Doran** (Albert), **Mike Starr** (Ducky), **Shelly Burch** (Jerrilyn).
*THE GENERAL:*
**Drew Barrymore** (Our Girl), **Candy Clark** (Sally Ann), **James Naughton** (Hugh).

PRODUCTION COMPANY:
**Famous Films/De Laurentiis/MGM/UA**

PRODUCER:
**Martha J. Schumacher**

CO-PRODUCER:
**Milton Subotsky**

SCREENPLAY:
**Stephen King**; *QUITTERS INC* and *THE LEDGE* are based on stories from his *Night Shift* collection.

Photographer: **Jack Cardiff**. Editor: **Scott Conrad**. Production designer: **Giorgio Postiglione**. Art director: **Jeffrey Ginn**. Sound: **Donald Summer**. Music: **Alan Silvestri**. Costumes: **Clifford Capone**. Make-up: **Sandi Duncan**. Special visual effects: **Barry Nolan**. Special effects co-ordinator: **Jeff Jarvis**. Creatures created by: **Carlo Rambaldi**. Models: **Emilio Ruiz**. Stunt co-ordinator: **Glenn Randall Jnr**. Animal action: **Karl Lewis Miller**. Technicolor. Cinemascope. Dolby stereo.

RUNNING TIME:
**94 mins**

■ 'Dr' Donatti, head of 'Quitters Inc.', guarantees that Morrison (centre) will stop smoking. He 'employs' the cooperation of Morrison's wife: watching her being electrocuted does wonders for his client's motivation.

## SPOT THE [K]IN[G] JOKES

A goodly number of the personnel involved in *CAT'S EYE* had been together in previous 'King' movies. Top of the list, of course, were King himself, 'impressario' Dino De Laurentiis (*THE DEAD ZONE* (1983), *FIRESTARTER* (1984)), director Lewis Teague (*CUJO*(1983)), producer Martha Schumacher (who had been assistant producer on *FIRESTARTER*) and actress Drew Barrymore (also *FIRESTARTER*). There were also repeat collaborations by production designer Giorgio Postiglione, special-effects co-ordinator Jeff Jarvis and stunt co-ordinator Glenn Randall (all from *FIRESTARTER*), and by animal trainer Karl Lewis Miller (from *CUJO*). Perhaps, then, it is not so surprising that in-jokes started to creep into the show. The ones too easy to score points with are:

• At the film's outset, the cat is attacked by a rabid St Bernard. FILM ?

• Cat's life No. 2 is almost lost when it's nearly run over by a '58 Plymouth Fury. FILM ?

• 'I don't know who writes this crap!' says Morrison in *QUITTERS, INC.* as he watches a movie on TV in which a guy has emerged from a coma with psychic powers. FILM?

• Our Girl's mother Sally Ann, in *THE GENERAL*, is reading a good thriller in which a man discovers by trial and error that 'Sometimes dead is better'. FILM?

Can you remember any others?

Laurentiis when he wants something — and he did have in mind a story idea that could be tailored for Drew... Thus Stephen King found himself producing the screenplay for *CAT'S EYE*. Director Lewis Teague read King's script — and found it very funny. He was pleased with the idea of working with King again, and with the opportunity to show that he could handle humour as well as horror.

DIGEM, which is the 'Director's Indispensable Guide to Effortless Moviemaking', opens its 'Avoid at All Costs!' page with 1: Children; 2: Animals; 3: Special-Effects. *CAT'S EYE* majors in each category. The *CAT'S EYE* stories demanded a considerable

array of impressive effects. In *QUITTERS, INC.* there was the 'electrocution chamber', a glassed-in room with a wire mesh floor which, when activated, leaves its unlucky occupants (in this case first the cat and then Morrison's wife) jumping and sparking. However, a great deal of the effects work here went into 'optical duplicity'; the film-makers repeatedly stressed that no cat had received any electric shocks.

*THE LEDGE* called for the amazing eye of perspectives-expert Emilio Ruiz. The ledge itself (around the 30-floor-high apartment block) was constructed a mere seven feet off the floor. To make the plight of Norris convincing, as he inches his way around the building — further endangered by high winds, pigeons and a hose-pipe wielded by Cressner — Ruiz devised a series of extraordinarily angled miniature buildings which, when they were positioned at the right distances from one another, perfectly recreated the Atlantic City skyline from Norris's viewpoint. 'This technique is unheard of today. It is a part of a bygone Hollywood,' said Lewis Teague.

Among the most entertaining of the special effects was the heartless, red-eyed, razor-toothed little gremlin (about six inches tall) who, in *THE GENERAL*, bursts through the walls into the child's bedroom with his tiny sword, scampering over the bed and battling with the cat. Special-effects maestro Carlo Rambaldi (the creator of *E.T.* (1982)) devised a ferocious head for 'The Troll': a complex mass of cables and levers permitted it to leer and snarl, his monstrous face crowned by a little jester's hat, complete with bells. Three tiny actors took turns to don the Troll costume. Small though they were, this necessitated a special duplicate set of Our Girl's bedroom, as seen from a Troll's-eye view. That meant reproducing everything in the room six times larger.

Constructing the oversized bedroom took 20 people five weeks to do, and it was estimated to have cost $150,000. Our Girl's desk grew (all measurements are here approximate) to 23ft long and 15ft wide. A doorknob became 15in in diameter; and her record albums expanded to 8ft square.

The *piece-de-resistance*, however, was Our Girl's bed. It had to be 41ft long and 21ft wide. The foot-end was 16ft high, and the top of the headboard stood at 21ft. The pillows were each 12ft long by 8ft wide. Most of the furniture in the room could only be moved by using a fork-lift truck. The bed earned itself a place in the *Guinness Book of Records*.

Drew Barrymore as the child was certainly one of the film's plus-factors. She had 'grown up' up a lot since her *FIRESTARTER* days when, as King said, she had had 'a terminal case of cute'.

As for the cat, sixteen moggies were 'hired' for use in the role, although three of them did most of the work. Animal-handler Karl Lewis Miller has explained that you train a dog to do tricks but you can only con a cat to perform. Cats aren't nearly as keen on doing things to please people as dogs are.

The cat had far more of a co-ordinating role in the movie as it was originally filmed. Lewis Teague had shot a prologue which began with Our Girl's funeral. Her grief-stricken mother, Sally Ann, is convinced that the cat did steal the child's breath.

She arms herself with a handy machine-gun and goes after the cat, who is even at that point trying to hunt down the Troll. The cat escapes — and sets off on its journey. This prologue explained why Our Girl appears to the cat in a vision begging the cat to 'Find it before it's too late' — 'it' being the murderous Troll. However, the film's backers were unhappy about the child's being dead at the outset of the film, and also how cat-lovers might react to the animal being shot at. Consequently, many of the feline star's finest scenes were left on the cutting-room floor.

■ In trying to reach Our Girl, in response to her cry for help, Our Cat has lost several of its lives. His final hurdle is the girl's mother, who can't see the evil little Troll, and thinks that the cat is the problem.

**The Films of Stephen King**

# Silver Bullet 1985

DIRECTOR:
**Daniel Attias**
*(USA, 1985)*

LEADING PLAYERS:
**Gary Busey** (Uncle Red),
**Corey Haim** (Marty Coslaw),
**Megan Follows** (Jane
Coslaw), **Everett McGill**
(Reverend Lowe), **Terry
O'Quinn** (Sheriff Haller),
**Robin Groves** (Nan Coslaw),
**Leon Russom** (Bob Coslaw),
**Bill Smitrovich** (Andy
Fairton), **Joe Wright** (Brady
Kincaid), **Kent Broadhurst**
(Herb Kincaid), **Heather
Simmons** (Tammy
Sturmfuller), **James A.
Baffico** (Milt Sturmfuller),
**Rebecca Fleming** (Mrs
Sturmfuller), **Lawrence
Tierney** (Owen Knopfler).

PRODUCTION COMPANY:
**International Film
Corporation**

PRODUCER:
**Martha Schumacher**

SCREENPLAY:
**Stephen King**; based on his
own novelette *Cycle Of The
Werewolf.*

Photographer: **Armando
Nannuzzi**. Editor: **Daniel
Lowenthal**. Production
designer: **Giorgio
Postiglione**. Sound: **Richard
Goodman**. Music: **Jay
Chattaway**. Costume
designer: **Clifford Capone**.
Creature creation: **Carlo
Rambaldi**. Special-effects
co-ordinator: **Joseph P.
Mercurio**. Special-effects
make-up: **Michael
McCracken Jnr**. Stunt co-
ordinator: **Julius LeFlore**.
**Technicolor. J-D-C
Widescreen.**

RUNNING TIME:
**95 mins**

*By the light of the
silvery moon, things
can get hairy!*

Every month when the moon was full, It came back - Its only Fear was the ... Silver Bullet.

STEPHEN KING'S

*Silver Bullet*

### SYNOPSIS

Jane Coslaw is
remembering a year
in her childhood —
1976 — in the little
town of Tarker's Mills,
Maine. [Then] She and
her younger brother
Marty quarrel a lot.
She feels he gets all
her parents' attention because he is
crippled and confined to a wheelchair. Also, Marty can be a mean
practical joker.

Unexplained deaths begin to
occur in the town. Marty and Jane
suspect a werewolf. They confide in
their much-loved Uncle Red — the
boozy black sheep of the family. The
townsfolk decide a psychopath is at
large, and form a vigilante group —
several of which are killed.

At a Fourth of July barbecue,
Marty goes off by himself in the new
motorized wheelchair (called the
'Silver Bullet') that Uncle Red has
designed for him. As he is setting off
his fireworks, the werewolf attacks
him, but Marty fires off a rocket
which hits it in the eye. The following day, Jane discovers the town
preacher, Reverend Lowe, wearing
an eyepatch. Marty, Jane and Uncle
Red persuade Sheriff Haller to investigate; he witnesses Reverend Lowe
turning into a wolf — but Haller is
killed. Red gets the local gunsmith
to turn Marty and Jane's St
Christopher medals into a silver
bullet. On Halloween, Reverend
Lowe-turned-werewolf breaks into
the Coslaw house. Marty shoots him
dead. Jane and Marty emerge from
their adventure knowing that they
care about each other.

**Many moons ago,** Stephen King was
asked to write material for a calendar. It
was to be a story in twelve instalments,
each of which would be illustrated by
the artist Bernie Wrightson. What could
be more 12-part and calendar-
connected than the phases of the
moon? And what could be more moon-
connected, for a writer of horror
fiction, than the cycles of a werewolf?
However, the stories grew too long for
a calendar, becoming instead the
novelette *Cycle of the Werewolf,* on
which *SILVER BULLET* is based.

The traditional suspense avenues for
a werewolf movie follow either the
path of: a) there's a weird murderer
about — Oh, my goodness it's a werewolf — now, who can it be? Or, b)
Johnny's a werewolf who can't stop
himself committing grisly murders;
how long can he keep from (any
remaining) friends and lovers the fact
that it's him?

*SILVER BULLET* follows formula a).
Of course, having worked out in the
first five minutes that it's formula a),
the horror-film buff spends the next

five minutes (maximum!) sniffing out the least likely culprit — yes, there he is, the Reverend Lowe — and then contents himself with estimating how long it's going to take 'the common herd' to figure it out.

The Reverend Lowe is a very glamorous man of the cloth. How he first became a werewolf is never explained. He has nightmares and hallucinations, in which those attending his church services turn into werewolves, too. The special-effects team made a careful distinction between the 'dream' werewolves, which were created by Michael McCracken Jr, and Carlo Rambaldi's 'creature' designs for Everett McGill as Lowe, which were unique although, some felt, rather more ursine than lupine.

The film's crippled-child hero was handled with delicacy. Nothing 'heavy' was made of it, and his relationship with his Uncle Red provided the film's emotional backbone. Gary Busey's portrayal of Uncle Red was one of the film's highlights.

One of the main problems in *SILVER BULLET* was the population of Tarker's Mills. As stupid towns in movies go, it may well take the biscuit. They pay scant attention to the murders at first, which — after all — only happen once a month. Vigilante posses pursue maniacs into misty woods. The Sheriff can only manage to call on the Reverend after dark. When the Fourth of July town party is wisely called off, the Coslaws set out on a little barbecue of their own. And finally, the hitherto overprotective Coslaw parents pick this time to go on holiday, leaving Marty and Jane in care of their pixilated uncle.

The film opens to Jane's voice proclaiming (sincerely) as she looks back on the mid-1970s: 'Tarker's Mill was a town where people cared about each other as much as they cared about themselves.' In that case, they needed a lesson in self-esteem.

■ Captivated by a sky full of glorious fireworks, Marty doesn't notice he's being crept up on, until it's almost too late.

## KING ON SILVER BULLET

'I can remember sitting in a room with Dino De Laurentiis and saying, "Does America need another werewolf story?" And Dino replied, "Oh, Stephen! Dey'll love it! Ees fantastic idea!" Well,' King concluded, 'it wasn't a fantastic idea, but I was charged with the idea of casting Gary Busey as the feisty, drunken uncle.'

*(From an interview with Stephen King, by Gary Wood, published in* Cinefantastique *magazine, February 1991.)*

## WOULD IT WERE A WOLF

The lycanthrope — the human who turns into a ravaging wolf at the full moon — is a mythological figure of lengthy lineage. Cinema cottoned onto it as early as 1913, in the 18-minute *THE WEREWOLF* — who was actually a woman, a Navajo medicine-woman's daughter. The next to 'out' as a Wolf Man was Henry Hull in Universal's *THE WEREWOLF OF LONDON* (1934). Lon Chaney Jnr didn't come howling onto the scene until 1941 in *THE WOLF MAN*.

One of the films Stephen King credits with having a major impact on kids of the 1950s was *I WAS A TEENAGE WEREWOLF* (1957). It starred Michael Langdon as a teenager sent to a psychiatrist to cure his ferocious rages. The psychiatrist regresses the boy — in the interests of his own research. Langdon thereupon contacts the primeval beast in himself — and a werewolf is born.

For King and his adolescent peers in the 1950s: 'Langdon became the fascinating embodiment of everything you're not supposed to do ... Langdon grows hair all over his face, produces long fangs, and begins to drool a substance that looks suspiciously like Burma-Shave ... here's a fellow who doesn't give a fart in a high wind for the Scholastic Aptitude Tests. He has gone ... not apeshit, but wolfshit.'

The werewolf syndrome lapsed largely for the next couple of decades, but the 1980s brought in a new pack. *SILVER BULLET* had been preceded by *THE HOWLING* (1980), *AN AMERICAN WEREWOLF IN LONDON* (1981), *WOLFEN* (1981), and *THE COMPANY OF WOLVES* (1984). Special-effects experts looked like being set for a rich career in wolf-work alone.

(From an interview with Stephen King, by Gary Wood, in *Cinefantastique* magazine, January 1986.)

■ If a small boy had defended himself by firing a rocket into your eyes, then wearing an eyepatch in the daylight hours would seem a dead giveaway. But it appears that the Reverend Lowe isn't a very bright werewolf.

# Maximum Overdrive 1986

*Machines are taking over! They're running by themselves! They're mad! They're — aaargggh ...*

## SYNOPSIS

**P**lanet Earth has just passed through the tail of a comet, and, in Wilmington, North Carolina, things start to go wrong. Machines begin to kill people. Out on the highway, big diesel trucks are smashing into cars. Young honeymooners Connie and Curt flee from the marauding vehicles into the Dixie Boy Truck Stop, where they are soon joined by others seeking sanctuary.

Henderson, the Dixie Boy's owner, is giving his short-order cook Bill Robinson a hard time. Bill is on parole from the local penitentiary, and Henderson is threatening that he will return him to the pen if he doesn't agree to work extra hours 'off the clock'.

However, the truck stop also comes under machine attack. A waitress is cut by an electric carving knife, and a soda machine fires cans

■ Parolee Bill Robinson relaxes against a seemingly innocent 'Happy Toyz' truck. But soon Robinson will have to outwit this Green Goblin, leader of a brigade of driverless trucks that lay siege to the Dixie Boy Truck Stop.

at people. Soon the Dixie Boy is surrounded by trucks 'demanding' that they be filled with petrol.

Bill manages to keep the killer convoy at bay with a rocket launcher which he finds in Henderson's basement. However, realising that they must escape before they run out of ammunition, the Dixie Boy's occupants manage to get away by making their way through a sewer passage into a road-side ditch, whence they head off in search of help and safety.

**D**ino De Laurentiis believed that the commercial failure of *CAT'S EYE* (1985) and *SILVER BULLET* (1985) was due to the insufficient hands-on control during film-making by Stephen King. So after he had persuaded King to write a screenplay for his short story 'Trucks', he then suggested that King direct it himself. King protested for a while, but then agreed, 'For a long time I thought maybe I ought to direct

an adaptation of one of my stories, because so many people have said to me that the film didn't seem like the book ... I was intensely curious to find out if I could translate whatever was in my heart and brain, the stuff that's between the lines, onto film.'

King confesses that he's frightened by machines, and loved the idea of making a movie about machines going crazy. And so he bravely sat down

DIRECTOR:
**Stephen King**
*(USA, 1986)*

LEADING PLAYERS:
**Emilio Estevez** (Bill Robinson), **Pat Hingle** (Henderson), **Laura Harrington** (Brett), **Yeardley Smith** (Connie), **John Short** (Curt), **Ellen McElduff** (Wanda June), **J.C. Quinn** (Duncan), **Christopher Murney** (Camp Loman), **Holter Graham** (Deke).

PRODUCTION COMPANY:
**Dino De Laurentiis Productions**

PRODUCER:
**Martha Schumacher**

CO-PRODUCER:
**Milton Subotsky**

SCREENPLAY:
**Stephen King,** from his short story 'Trucks', from the *Night Shift* collection.

Photographer: **Armando Nannuzzi**. Editor: **Evan Lottman**. Production designer: **Giorgio Postiglione**. Art director: **Rod Schumacher**. Sound: **Ed White**. Music: **AC/DC**. Costume design: **Clifford Capone**. Special effects make-up: **Dean Gates**. Special effects co-ordinator: **Steve Galick**. Special visual effects supervisor: **Barry Nolan**. Stunt co-ordinator: **Glenn Randall Jnr**. Technicolor. **J-D-C Widescreen. Dolby stereo.**

RUNNING TIME:
**97 mins**

behind a potentially eye-exploding camera and got to work.

He soon found out how little he knew. He remembers the first occasion on which one of his instructions was greeted by the crew members looking at one another in silent disbelief: 'It

■ The shock that cheery waitress Wanda June gets when an electric knife attacks her is but a quiet start to a day that turns out to be full of renegade coffee pots, toasters and soft-drink machines.

was like farting at a dinner party,' he recalls. He remembers, too, that even when they explained why his request was cinematographically impossible — he didn't understand them. He would return home at the end of the day and phone his friend, the director George Romero, who would roar with laughter at King's plight, but who would then help all that he could.

The main problem for King the Director seems to have been that although King the Scriptwriter had proved, in the past, to be an extremely co-operative and creative colleague for experienced directors who knew exactly what they needed, he wasn't a great deal of help to an inexperienced director who knew what he wanted, but who didn't know what it took to make that possible.

King decided that he wanted to create a 'moron movie': one which was fast, vulgar and violent; one which didn't have a lot of dialogue, and that which there was was pretty profane. To this end, he didn't spend a lot of time developing his characters. Pat Hingle's Henderson comes across as the very epitome of screen nastiness; Emilio Estevez's Bill Robinson is disillusioned and unengaging; and most of the other members of the cast have roles that portray either 'good old guys' or hysterics.

Although there are too many illogicalities to make suspension of disbelief easy in *MAXIMUM OVERDRIVE* (why some rebellious machines and not others? And why murderous trucks and not cars?), there is a satisfyingly outrageous array of berserk-machine attacks: a personal stereo blows up its listener's ears; a power-mower dices its operator; a heavily trafficked drawbridge-road opens under its own steam; a dog is killed by the toy car it has been 'worrying'; and a blood-stained ice-cream truck patrols the streets tinkling 'King of the Road'. King himself has a cameo role as a man using a roadside automatic bank-teller which uses its new-found liberation to inform him, 'You're an asshole!'

### KING ON MAXIMUM OVERDRIVE

*'I didn't do a very good job of directing it. I didn't have a lot of production support from the De Laurentiis organization which, by that time, was beginning to get on extremely thin ice financially ... MAXIMUM OVERDRIVE was for me ... a crash course in film school. What some guys take six years to learn, I learned in about ten weeks. The result was a picture that was just terrible. But it had some things in it that make me think, "Well, I can go back and I can do it right the second time. Now I understand."'*

(From an interview with Stephen King, by Gary Wood, in Cinefantastique magazine, February 1991.)

## THE KING MEETS THE ROMAN EMPEROR

Dino De Laurentiis (the man responsible for the making of *THE DEAD ZONE (1983)*, *FIRESTARTER (1984)*, *CAT'S EYE (1985)*, *SILVER BULLET (1985)* and *MAXIMUM OVERDRIVE*) was born in Italy in 1919. He has trodden a sure-footed path since an early age. He moved into the family pasta business at 14, left it at 17 to become an actor, quickly decided that film-producing was a better bet, and went on to make some classic Italian movies, including *LA STRADA (1954)* and *NIGHTS OF CABIRIA (1957)*. He moved into epics and big international co-productions, including *ULYSSES (1955)*, *WAR AND PEACE (1956)* and *BARBARELLA (1968)*. He built his own Italian studios, modestly named Dinocitta, and by 1980 had the largest film-producing organization in Europe.

During the 1970s, he also opened a production company in the USA. His steady output of movies included *KING KONG (1976)*, *FLASH GORDON (1980)*, *RAGTIME (1981)*, *CONAN THE BARBARIAN (1982)* and *THE BOUNTY (1983)*.

In 1981, De Laurentiis purchased the rights to *THE DEAD ZONE*. A strong relationship between Dino and King quickly developed. Said Debra Hill, producer of *THE DEAD ZONE*, 'I think Dino has a real respect for Stephen, a real true love of the man, of working with him. He gave Stephen the opportunity not only to sell the rights to his books, but to write screenplays, and direct them as well.'

*CAT'S EYE* was the first film shot in De Laurentiis's new studios in Wilmington, North Carolina. The studios went bankrupt a few years later, but De Laurentiis moved on to open Paradise Films in California.

Apart from *THE DEAD ZONE*, De Laurentiis's films of King's books are among the least successful. Why did King stay with him so long? 'The answer is,' says King, 'he's a very persuasive man. He's hypnotic. He's magnetic. He's still one of the most fabulous creatures that I've ever met in my life. He's seductive. So I went on.'

(From interviews with Debra Hill and Stephen King, by Gary Wood in *Cinefantastique*, February 1991.)

■ The trucks go into maximum overdrive, slewing out of control as they run people down, smash into cars, crash into buildings, overturn and explode. Director Stephen King had a lovely time blowing things up.

**The Films of Stephen King**

# Stand By Me 1986

DIRECTOR:
**Rob Reiner**
*(USA, 1986)*

LEADING PLAYERS:
**Wil Wheaton** (Gordie Lachance), **River Phoenix** (Chris Chambers), **Corey Feldman** (Teddy Duchamp), **Jerry O'Connell** (Vern Tessio), **Richard Dreyfuss** (the writer/adult Gordie), **Kiefer Sutherland** (Ace Merrill), **Casey Siemaszko** (Billy Tessio), **Gary Riley** (Charlie Hogan), **Bradley Gregg** (Eyeball Chambers), **Jason Oliver** (Vince Desjardins), **Marshall Bell** (Mr Lachance), **Frances Lee McCain** (Mrs Lachance), **Bruce Kirby** (Mr Quidacioluo), **William Bronder** (Milo Pressman), **Scott Beach** (Mayor Grundy), **John Cusack** (Denny Lachance).

PRODUCTION COMPANY:
**Act III Productions/ Columbia Pictures**

PRODUCERS:
**Andrew Scheinman, Bruce A. Evans, Raynold Gideon**

SCREENPLAY:
**Raynold Gideon, Bruce A. Evans**; based on the novella 'The Body' by **Stephen King**.

Photographer: **Thomas Del Ruth**. Editor: **Robert Leighton**. Production designer: **Dennis Washington**. Sound: **Bob Eber**, (music) **Mark Curry**. Music: **Jack Nitzsche**; theme song 'Stand By Me': **B.E. King, J. Leiber, M. Stoller**, performed by **B.E. King**. Costume supervisor: **Sue Moore**. Make-up: **Monty Westmore**. Special effects: **Richard L. Thompson, Henry Millar**. Stunt co-ordinator: **Rick Barker**. Technicolor; prints by **DeLuxe**.

RUNNING TIME:
**89 mins**

*'I was twelve going on thirteen the first time I saw a dead human being'*

"A MAGICAL AND WHOLLY DELIGHTFUL SURPRISE."
DEREK MALCOLM (THE GUARDIAN—GREAT BRITAIN)

"A gripping story about growing up which brings back memories of one's own youth...Entertaining and well made."
HARALD STOFFELS (BILD—GERMANY)

"A wonderful movie with remarkable performances."
JULIE SALOMON (WALL STREET JOURNAL—USA)

"...such superb acting that you will leave the theatre with a feeling that you have really experienced something."
MATS OLSSON (EXPRESSEN—SWEDEN)

"...excellent performances...is a little gem...anybody who likes good movies, can't afford to miss this one."
JORGE CAMARA (EL HERALDO—MEXICO)

"My favourite movie of the year."
JONATHAN KING (BBC TELEVISION—GREAT BRITAIN)

"A marvellous, engaging adventure about boyhood revisited that evokes memories of that exciting but difficult time on the brink of teenagehood...superb performances."
JOHN HANRAHAN (THE SYDNEY SUN—AUSTRALIA)

"A haunting coming-of-age film that mixes quirky humour, menace and pathos in an absolutely original fashion."
STEPHEN FARBER (NEW YORK TIMES—USA)

**STAND BY ME.**
A new film by Rob Reiner

A ROB REINER FILM "STAND BY ME" STARRING WIL WHEATON RIVER PHOENIX COREY FELDMAN JERRY O'CONNELL KIEFER SUTHERLAND MUSIC JACK NITZSCHE DIRECTOR OF PHOTOGRAPHY THOMAS DEL RUTH SCREENPLAY RAYNOLD GIDEON & BRUCE A. EVANS BASED UPON THE NOVELLA "THE BODY" BY STEPHEN KING PRODUCED BY BRUCE A. EVANS RAYNOLD GIDEON AND ANDREW SCHEINMAN DIRECTED BY ROB REINER
COLUMBIA PICTURES PRESENTS AN ACT III PRODUCTION
RELEASED BY COLUMBIA-CANNON-WARNER DISTRIBUTORS LIMITED

## SYNOPSIS

Gordie Lachance, a writer, is remembering back 25 years to 1959, in Castle Rock, when he was 12-years-old. His friend Vern's brother Billy is overheard saying he's seen the body of a missing teenager in the woods. Vern and Gordie, and mates Teddy and Chris decide to find the corpse, and hope this will get their pictures in the papers. Chris takes along his father's .45 pistol.

The four boys have a series of adventures: Gordie is nearly caught by the local dump's guard dog; they play 'race the train' across a high trestle bridge and are almost run over; they camp out for the night, and get very scared until Gordie distracts them with a story. The next day, they go swimming in a pool, and come out covered in leeches.

Just when Verne spots the body in the grass, Billy and the other town thugs, led by Ace Merrill, drive up to claim the corpse. Everything looks pretty desperate until Gordie produces the pistol, at which point the gang drives off. The boys then return to Castle Rock without the body (the police are later informed anonymously).

Grown-up Gordie's memories have been revived on learning that Chris had been killed while trying to quieten a brawl in a bar, and he has been writing his recollections of that last summer of childhood into a story. Now he's finished it, and goes outside to play with his own kids.

**R**ob Reiner happened into *STAND BY ME* almost accidentally. The scriptwriters asked him for a 'friendly' opinion of their screenplay, and he found himself so intrigued by the story that he sat down to read the original — 'The Body', in Stephen King's *Different Seasons* collection. Reiner thereafter let it be known that if the already chosen director, Adrien Lynne, was unable to do it for any reason, then he — Reiner — would be eager to take over. And that's exactly how things worked out. 'Initially what attracted me,' Reiner

recalls, 'was the intelligence of the writing in the original story — the characters were very well drawn.'

At the same time he was looking to do something more dramatic, something different from the things he had done in the past [the spoof rockumentary *THIS IS SPINAL TAP* (1984), and the romantic comedy *THE SURE THING*, (1985). 'I called the author [King] because I assumed that the piece was semi-autobiographical, or at least gave some hints as to what led to him becoming a writer. I asked him

how much of it was true. And he said, "Well, to be honest with you, I'm a pathological liar, and I don't know what is and what isn't true, but if it isn't true, it should be!"'

Reiner also felt his own personal connections with the story, it being about '...a youth who feels he's not understood, with a lot of doubts and fears about himself, who through the help of a friend starts to feel good and have confidence in himself. For both King and myself the story was a lot more than just four boys searching the woods for a body.'

The story examines a time of great change for Gordie, Chris, Teddy and Vern through a powerful rites-of-passage tale. They are at one of the first great turning-points of their lives, after which nothing will ever be quite the same again. They will, at the end of the summer, all be going on to junior high school, and they won't be in the same class as each other any more. Gordie will study for college; the others will train for blue-collar jobs.

However, Gordie's braininess doesn't mean that, compared to the others, life for him is a picnic. Not so long ago, his big brother Denny was killed in a car crash. Denny was bright, athletic, popular, kind — Gordie's hero. His mother still constantly grieves, and his father is unable to hide the fact that he wishes it had been Gordie who had died instead.

Chris, in theory the 'tough guy' of the group, is very sensitive to Gordie's loneliness and rejection. He is sensible, protective and highly supportive of Gordie's wish to be a writer. Chris comes from 'the wrong side of the tracks' and has a criminally inclined family and an otherwise unwarranted bad reputation. He did, indeed, steal some school milk money, but felt guilty enough to confess and return it to a teacher; she kept the money, and allowed him to be branded a thief.

Teddy's father was shell-shocked in World War II to the point that Teddy suffered much at his hands before his father was deemed 'certifiable'. Now

■ Tearaway Teddy (far left) is restrained by Chris (centre) from stoning the train that nearly ran him and Gordie down. The two boys had double-dared themselves to cross a bridge before a train caught them, and they had only just made it...

## S.O.S. — SAVE OUR STORY

It is the closing moments of the movie. Grown-up Gordie's voice (by courtesy of Richard Dreyfuss) has been with us throughout the film, commenting on the adventures of the summer. Now we're looking at grown-up Gordie, sitting in front of his word processor and we realise that he did become a writer, and even as he's been recalling and recounting the story, he's been typing it onto his computer. Dreyfuss/Gordie writes his final lines, 'I never had any friends later on like the ones I had when I was 12. Jesus, did anyone?'

Well satisfied with the job, Dreyfuss/Gordie leans forward, stretches out an arm and something clicks off. In cinemas all over the world, regular users of word processors go into shock. Some even call out — 'Save it!' He didn't save it! He only made one movement where there should have been two — a 'saving' movement and a 'switching-off' movement. It's gone! The story's been wiped out!

Nonsense, said Reiner. As Dreyfuss/Gordie finished his story, the shot showed him seated; the next showed him standing up. Why wouldn't he have pushed the 'save' button before he switched off? After all, pushing a 'save' button doesn't make any noise.

It's alright in theory, Mr Reiner, but it wasn't alright in practice.

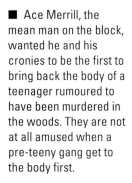

■ Ace Merrill, the mean man on the block, wanted he and his cronies to be the first to bring back the body of a teenager rumoured to have been murdered in the woods. They are not at all amused when a pre-teeny gang get to the body first.

Teddy has to contend with taunts of 'Your father's in the loony bin'. Teddy compensates for such slights by constantly putting himself on the line.

Vern is pudgy and slow and scared. Everyone pokes fun at Vern — but at least he knows he's safe with his three best schoolmates. That doesn't mean to say he's immune from verbal attack. The boys bounce along the woodland paths insulting everything they can about each other. Their language was, in fact, so colourful and so true to the way teenagers speak that it was certified unfit for said teenagers to watch.

Of the films of King's books and stories up to that time, *STAND BY ME* got closest to both his words and the feelings between his lines. All the joys and pitfalls of boys growing up in small-town America were retained; all the painful paradoxes of family life. And the emotional complexity of boys of that age was richly explored: sex talk, profanity, tears, giggles, dares, jeering, sharing, risks, fears.

Such was the gentle innocence of the movie that it was deemed wiser, as far as possible, to keep Stephen King's name out of it: had the film been titled Stephen King's *THE BODY* after the novella on which it was based, it would have brought in the wrong crowd. King agreed, so it became *STAND BY ME*. King's name was 'quietly' inserted in the film's credits.

So, ironically, at the same time as the well-publicized *MAXIMUM OVERDRIVE (1986)* was failing to prove itself to be the definitive 'King movie', Reiner's little sleeper was packing them in and even pushing *TOP GUN* (1986) off the top of the box-office charts.

## REINER ON KING

*'I was very nervous because I wanted him [King] to like it. I didn't actually watch the film with him. I showed up after it was over and ran into him. He was visibly moved … He said, "Listen, I've got to compose myself. I'll come back and talk to you." He came back in about 15 to 20 minutes and we sat and talked. He said this was by far the best film that had ever been made out of any of his works.'*

(From an interview with Rob Reiner, by Gary Wood, published in Cinefantastique, February 1991.)

■ During the confrontation between the four friends and Merrill's gang in the woods, the young heroes win out. However, later on Ace catches up with Chris…

# Creepshow 2 1987

## DIRECTOR:
**Michael Gornick**
*(USA, 1987)*

## LEADING PLAYERS:
*OLD CHIEF WOOD'NHEAD:*
**George Kennedy** (Ray Spruce), **Dorothy Lamour** (Martha Spruce), **Don Harvey** (Andy Cavenaugh), **David Holbrook** (Fatso Gribbens), **Holt McCallany** (Sam Whitemoon), **Frank S. Salsedo** (Ben Whitemoon), **Maltby Napoleon** (1st Indian), **Tyrone Tonto** (2nd Indian), **Dan Kamin** (Old Chief Wood'nhead), **Deane Smith** (Mr Cavenaugh), **Shirley Sonderegger** (Mrs Cavenaugh).
*THE RAFT:*
**Daniel Beer** (Randy), **Jeremy Green** (Laverne), **Page Hannah** (Rachel), **Paul Satterfield** (Deke).
*THE HITCHHIKER:*
**Lois Chiles** (Annie Lansing), **Stephen King** (truck-driver), **Tom Wright** (hitchhiker), **David Beecroft** (Annie's lover), **Richard Parks** (George Lansing), **Cheré Bryson** (woman at accident).
*Linking Sequences:*
**Tom Savini** (The Creep), **Domenick John** (Billy), **Philip Doré** (Curly), **Joe Silver** (voice of The Creep).

## PRODUCTION COMPANY:
**Laurel Productions/New World Pictures**

## PRODUCER:
**David Ball**

## SCREENPLAY:
**George A Romero**; based on the short stories by **Stephen King**, including 'The Raft' from his *Night Shift* collection.

Photographers: **Richard Hart, Tom Hurwitz**. Editor: **Peter Weatherly**. Production designer: **Bruce Miller**.

*Watch out!*
*Watch out!*
*The Creep's about!*

## SYNOPSIS

*WRAP-AROUND STORY:* Once again, the wrap-around story holds the different stories together. Young Billy waits at the news-stand to buy the first *Creepshow* comic off the stacks. And there is The Creep waiting to introduce his newest tales of horror.

*OLD CHIEF WOOD'NHEAD:* Times are hard in Dead River. The local reservation Indians, led by Ben Whitemoon, come to the General Store to ask its kindly proprietors, Ray and Martha Spruce, whether they will accept some of the tribe's precious jewellery as security against their ever-increasing debt. That night the couple are viciously attacked and killed by young Sam Whitemoon and two hoodlum cronies, who steal the jewels. The old wooden cigar-store Indian chief 'awakens' and goes after the hood-lums. When Ben Whitemoon returns the following day, the chief has the jewels in one hand and Sam's scalp in the other.

*THE RAFT:* Four college co-eds — Randy, Rachel, Deke and Laverne — swim out to a raft on a deserted lake for a swimming party. They notice something in the water that looks like the black blob of an oil slick, except it's moving towards them very fast. Rachel dips her hand into the 'oil', and is yanked into the water and gobbled up. Then a black filament snakes across the boards, grabs Deke's ankles and consumes him as it pulls him into the water. The blob then strikes at Laverne, eating her hair and face. Randy leaps into the water and, swimming madly, reaches the shore; but an oily wave crashes onto the beach and sweeps over him...

*THE HITCHHIKER:* Annie leaves her lover's house, driving her Mercedes fast in order to get home before her husband. She barely sees the hitchhiker before she hits and kills him. She drives away from his body — but then sees him standing in the road before her. Annie swerves and carries on, but next sees him above her, through the sun-roof. She takes a gun from the glove compartment and shoots him. As she parks the Mercedes in her garage, she hears the hitchhiker's voice thanking her for the ride.

*WRAP-AROUND STORY:* While The Creep has been telling his tales, little Billy has dropped in at the post-office to pick up a mail-order Venus Flytrap plant. Some local bullies then chase Billy to a deserted plot of land — not realising that this is Billy's private patch of giant Venus Flytraps which are waiting for lunch. As always, The Creep gets the last laugh.

**CREEPSHOW** did well enough at the box-office for Stephen King and the film's director George A. Romero to feel sure that backers would look quite favourably on a sequel. Over a period of time, and doubtless over many beers, various ideas were tossed around.

When it finally happened, in 1987, *CREEPSHOW 2* rather fell between two stools. The inter-linking tale's comic-style animated sections of horror stories leaping off *Creepshow*'s pages at the bidding of The Creep may well have provoked some fond nostalgia in an adult audience; yet, this fairly substantial wrap-around story of 11-year-old Billy versus the bully boys was very much of pre-adolescent interest. On the other hand, two of the three main episodes concerned an older and an elderly couple; and all three were peppered with gore, groping and god-awful language.

There seemed, too, to be a rather unfortunate and insidious moral tone to the whole proceedings: for violent young hoodlums (however deprived), for adulterous women (especially if sexually satisfied), and for pot-smoking, petting, party-loving teenagers, death is the only just reward. Look out! If you're not a model kid or a model wife, the Boogeyman will get you!

George Romero this time 'merely' wrote the screenplays for King's stories. *The Raft* was first published in the 'men's magazine', *Gallery*, before later finding a more respectable home in King's *Night Shift* collection; the other two tales were hitherto unpublished. Romero, a good friend of

Sound: **Felipe Borrero**. Music: **Les Reed**. Additional music: **Rick Wakeman**. Costume designer: **Eileen Sieff**. Make-up: **Joanna Robinson**. Make-up effects: **Howard Berger, Ed French**. Animation supervisor: **Rick Catizone**. Stunt co-ordinator: **Taso N. Stavrakis**. Technicolor.

RUNNING TIME: **89 mins**

■ Old-timer Ray Spuce has been painting a wooden Indian that stands outside his Dead River general store. The Indian can't thank him, but in due course he does avenge him.

THE MASTERS OF THE MACABRE
STEPHEN KING AND GEORGE A. ROMERO
WELCOME YOU TO

55

THE MASTERS OF THE MACABRE
STEPHEN KING AND GEORGE A. ROMERO
WELCOME YOU TO **CREEPSHOW 2** (18)

■ Annie's getting care-less: the hitchhiker she knocked over turned out to be the zombie sort who doesn't have the decency to stay dead.

Stephen King, is sensitive to the problems of transferring King's work satisfactorily to the screen, 'I think [King is] hard to adapt in what is thought of by the main-stream industry as a commercial way. It's hard to squeeze Steve's stuff into the kind of formula things that studios want and that, usually, audiences buy'.

Michael Gornick, long-time cameraman with George Romero and cinematographer of *CREEPSHOW*, here made his directorial debut. And Tom Savini, make-up-effects artist (on several Romero movies, including *CREEPSHOW*), this time stayed in front of the camera and let other hands turn him into The Creep. Stephen King did a 'Hitchcock', appearing as a truck-driver in *THE HITCHHIKER*. And *OLD CHIEF WOOD'NHEAD* featured a 'comeback': Dorothy Lamour, Hollywood's Queen of the South Sea Islands, hadn't been seen on a screen since more than a decade before in the TV movie *DEATH AT LOVE HOUSE* (1976).

The special effects called for were wide-ranging. There were the animated comic-comes-alive sequences; some excellent work in bringing Old Chief Wood'nhead to life; all the antics of *THE RAFT*'s malevolent oil puddle; and the free-wheeling, omnipresent, disintegrating zombie in *THE HITCHHIKER*.

With so many enthusiastic people putting their expertise into this enterprise, it produced fair measures of both fun and fearsome pleasure. Perhaps most entertainment was afforded by speculation as to the true nature of *THE RAFT*'s monster 'blob'. Film reviewers of the time varied widely in their interpretations.

A 'tarpaulin covered with black goo' was perhaps the least enterprising suggestion; a 'floating black-plastic bin-liner' was favoured by several contenders; 'man-eating plastic wrapping' was a promising entry; but the prize for the best answer had to go to 'man-eating oil slick'. This it clearly was; it even belched as it swallowed the last of its lunch.

## KING ON CREEPSHOW 2

'...There wasn't enough money... enough time, and still we came out with one piece that was good, THE HITCHHIKER ... Then you've got the one about the float [THE RAFT]. The oil-slick monster looked like some dirty old man's raincoat.'

( *Stephen King, interviewed by Gary Wood, published in* Cinefantastique, *February 1991.*)

# The Running Man

## 1987

*It's the ultimate live death game — and it's rigged...*

DIRECTOR:
**Paul Michael Glaser**
*(USA, 1987)*

LEADING PLAYERS:
**Arnold Schwarzenegger** (Ben Richards), **Maria Conchita Alonso** (Amber Mendez), **Yaphet Kotto** (Laughlin), **Jim Brown** (Fireball), **Jesse Ventura** (Captain Freedom), **Erland Van Lidth** (Dynamo), **Marvin J. McIntyre** (Weiss), **Gus Rethwisch** (Buzzsaw) **Professor Toru Tanaka** (Subzero), **Mich Fleetwood** (Mic), **Dweezil Zappa** (Stevie), **Richard Dawson** (Damon Killian).

PRODUCTION COMPANY:
**Taft-Barish Productions**

PRODUCERS:
**Tim Zinnemann, George Linder**

SCREENPLAY:
**Steven E. de Souza**; based on the novel by **Richard Bachman** [Stephen King]

Photographer: **Tom Del Ruth**. Editors: **Mark Roy Warner, Edward A. Warschilka, John Wright**. Production designer: **Jack T. Collis**. Sound: **Richard Bryce Goodman**. Music: **Harold Faltermeyer**. Costume designer: **Robert Blackman**. Key make-up: **Jefferson Dawn**. Special make-up effects: **The Burman Studio**. Special effects co-ordinator: **Larry Cavanaugh**. Special effects supervisor: **Bruce Sternheimer**. Special visual-effects supervisor: **Gary Gutierrez**. Stunt co-ordinator: **Bennie Dobbins**. Technicolor. Dolby stereo.

RUNNING TIME:
**101 mins**

## SYNOPSIS

It is the year 2019. And after the financial collapse of the USA, it is a police state. All TV news of protest groups is suppressed, and people are fed only mindless game shows.

During a food riot in Bakersfield, police helicopter pilot Ben Richards refuses to open fire on the crowd, but his crew overpower him and many rioters are killed. Richards is framed for the massacre, labelled 'The Butcher of Bakersfield', and imprisoned. After 18 months, he escapes with fellow convicts Laughlin and Weiss, but they are recaptured and then requisitioned by the No. 1 game-show host Damon Killian, who was impressed with their jail-break.

Killian wants them to take part in the top-rated 'The Running Man' show, in which weaponless contes-tants (all 'criminals') are pursued by heavily armoured Stalkers. Bets are placed by the TV audience. If a contestant succeeds in out-running the Stalkers, he wins his freedom plus luxurious prizes; if he doesn't — he dies. So far, no contestant has survived, and the TV audience is getting dangerously bored.

One by one the Stalkers are defeated by Richards, Laughlin and Weiss, who then link up with the People's Network resistance group. The TV audience begins to side with Richards, until Killian broadcasts a 'newsfilm' report of his death. However, the 'Running Men' and the freedom fighters break into the TV studio and broadcast proof of how dishonest the system is. Killian is killed by an explosion when he tries to prevent them.

*THE RUNNING MAN* is barely a Stephen King film. It was to have been directed by George Pan Cosmatos (of *RAMBO: FIRST BLOOD PART II* (1985)) and to have starred Christopher Reeve. Whether that movie would have differed from the Schwarzenegger vehicle that eventually hit the screens — we'll never know.

Direction of *THE RUNNING MAN* was begun by Andy Davis (*CODE OF SILENCE* (1985)), but he was replaced, early on, by Paul Michael 'Starsky' Glaser. Apart from his regular weekly starring role therein, Glaser had directed several episodes of *STARSKY AND HUTCH*, as well as the thriller *BAND OF THE HAND* (1986). Glaser certainly kept the action — all the battle and chase scenes — going at a cracking pace, and made sure that Arnie looked impressive at all times.

The film's outstanding performance came from Richard Dawson. In his role as Damon Killian, the heartless compere of 'The Running Man', the most popular TV game show ever, Dawson viciously sent up all such game-show hosts — including his own 8-year stint on *FAMILY FEUD* (*FAMILY FORTUNES* in the UK). Dawson/Killian gets all the good lines that haven't been allotted to Arnie, 'Get me the Justice Department, Entertainment Division,' he snaps. 'No — put me through to the President's agent.' However, the show's ratings have been slipping; the Stalkers never lose, so there's really no contest. Hence, Killian's interest in the bunch of guys who managed to escape from the country's most brutal and closely guarded prison; maybe they can add some new excitement.

Some of the movie's most telling moments centred on the reaction of

the film's TV studio audience to the show. The faces of those who are lucky enough to participate in the game register enormous pride and excitement as they pick the Stalker they wish to back: each time their 'hero' wastes another wimpy contestant, the lucky chooser wins a prize. The obvious gleeful enthusiasm of these vicarious killers is one of the few truly grim elements that can be traced — at least in spirit — back to Stephen King's original work.

*THE RUNNING MAN* interwove two film genres. There was the 'Death Game' movie (such as *THE MOST DEADLY GAME* (1932) or *DEATH RACE 2000* (1975)) merging with the 'City After the Apocalypse' genre (as in *THE WARRIORS* (1979) or *ESCAPE FROM NEW YORK* (1981)). In *THE RUNNING MAN*, L.A. had been wrecked by an earthquake back in 1996. Some 20 years later, L.A.'s urban-renewal scheme has clearly suffered several setbacks, but the city's ruins do make a great hunting ground in which the Stalkers are able to pursue their quarry.

■ TV game host Damon Killian getting a few final words from Ben Richards before he is launched from the TV studio to be hunted through earthquake-devastated L.A. (Only Arnie could look good in a sunshine-yellow satin jumpsuit with quilted sleeves.)

■ King's novel was extensively reworked for the screen as a vehicle for screen idol Arnold Schwarzenegger. The plot-line, therefore, came in well behind the action and effects, not to mention Arnie's pithy one-liners.

The film's Ben Richards has a better time of it than the novel's bleak hero who is risking his joyless life and soul to pay for the medicine his sick daughter needs. Arnie's Ben is a cop-with-a-conscience who's been betrayed by the system; a character audiences empathize with. He has a lovely lady, who starts out suspicious (and shops him), but recognizes his wonderful qualities in time to be of assistance. He aligns himself with the Cause of Democracy and pits his wits and muscles against impressive opponents.

The Stalkers feature nowhere in King's novel. They are the brain-child of scriptwriter Steven E. de Souza. Several of them are *bigger* than Arnie. Jesse Ventura, 'real-life' TV-wrestler and commentator, plays Captain Freedom, whose Stalker act includes a brand of killer aerobics. Jim Brown, former all-pro running-back for the Cleveland Browns, portrays Fireball the Flamethrower, who 'packs a little napalm in each fiery punch'. Weightlifter Gus Rethwisch is chain-saw-armoured Buzzsaw; however, Arnie slices him through the groin with his own chainsaw — and throws in the cheery aside, 'He had to split'.

Martial-arts master (and professional wrestler) Professor Toru Tanaka, weighing in at 350lbs, plays the role of Subzero, who is equipped with a razor-sharp hockey stick and some exploding pucks. Last but not least was the mighty Erland Van Lidth (another wrestler) playing the role of Dynamo. Not only does he laser-fry those who obstruct his path, he further shatters them with his rendering of operatic arias. Needless to say, none of this Superleague is up to Arnie.

## KING ON THE RUNNING MAN

'It was totally out of my hands. I didn't have anything to do with making it. They obviously saw it as a book that could be adapted to fit an existing **RAMBO/TERMINATOR** kind of genre, where you're able to give Schwarzenegger the tag lines that he's known for, like "I'll be back". The best thing about that was casting Richard Dawson as the game-show host. He was great. But the rest of it … doesn't have much in common with the novel at all, except the title.'

(From an interview with Stephen King, by Gary Wood, published in Cinefantastique, February 1991.)

# Pet Sematary 1989

DIRECTOR:
**Mary Lambert**
*(USA, 1989)*

LEADING PLAYERS:
**Dale Midkiff** (Louis Creed),
**Fred Gwynne** (Jud Crandall), **Denise Crosby** (Rachel Creed), **Brad Greenquist** (Victor Pascow), **Michael Lombard** (Irwin Goldman), **Blaze Berdahl** (Ellie Creed), **Miko Hughes** (Gage Creed), **Susan Blommaert** (Missy Dandridge), **Mara Clark** (Marcy Charlton), **Kavi Raz** (Steve Masterton), **Mary Louise Wilson** (Dory Goldman), **Andrew Hubatsek** (Zelda), **Matthew August Ferrell** (Jud as a child), **Lisa Stathoplos** (Jud's mother), **Stephen King** (minister), **Elizabeth Ureneck** (Rachel as a child), **Richard Collier** (young Jud), **Beau Berdahl** (Ellie Creed #2).

PRODUCTION COMPANY:
**Paramount Pictures**

PRODUCER:
**Richard P. Rubinstein**

CO-PRODUCER:
**Mitchell Galin**

*Be careful what you wish for — it might come true...*

## SYNOPSIS

Dr Louis Creed moves from Chicago with his family — wife Rachel, five-year-old Ellie, two-year-old Gage, and Church the cat — to an old house some way out of the little village of Ludlow in Maine. Their nearest neighbour is elderly Jud Crandall who warns Louis about the nearby juggernaut highway on which village pets are often killed — hence the nearby 'Pet Sematary'.

When Church is killed on the highway, Jud tells Louis to bury him in the Micmac Indian burial ground beyond the pet cemetery, which he does — even though he has been warned by the ghost of Victor, a fatally injured patient, not to go there. The next morning Church reappears, but with a new and vicious nature and a strange smell.

Shortly afterwards, Gage is killed on the highway. After the funeral his father digs up his body and reburies it on Micmac ground. Gage duly returns — brandishing a scalpel. He kills first Jud and then his mother before Louis manages to administer a lethal injection. Louis takes Rachel's body straight up to the burial ground, hoping he has been quick enough to resurrect her with both a healthy body and mind. Rachel does reappear, and he takes her in his arms, only to see that she is holding a knife...

■ Neighbour Jud Crandall knows about the ghoulish power of the ancient Micmac burial site beyond the pet 'sematary' (as scrawled in a child's hand), but he cautions Louis against using it, because, 'Sometimes dead is better'.

**S**tephen King's *Pet Sematary*, on being published, quickly became a No. 1 Bestseller: indeed, it remained on *Time* magazine's best-seller list for over 30 weeks. However, although the movie rights were snapped up quickly enough by Laurel Entertainment, with George Romero slated to direct, various obstacles appeared. Firstly, 1983 had already seen a rash of Stephen King movies — *CUJO* (1983), *THE DEAD ZONE* (1983) and

## THE ONE THAT NEARLY GOT AWAY

*For a long time, Stephen King couldn't bring himself to publish Pet Sematary. Even he was frightened by it. The story left him terror-struck, showing him levels of blackness in men's lives and beyond that he had no desire to revisit. 'I ended up,' he said, 'in perfect blackness.'*

*In 1980 (three years before it appeared) he said, 'It's done, but it's put away. I have no plans to publish it in the near future. It's too horrible... I gave it to my wife. She read two-thirds of it and — she's never done this before — she gave it back and said, "Why don't you go ahead and put it away?" I said, "Didn't you like it?" And she said, "There's no word for how I felt. I think it's effective... too effective."*

*'I got the idea when my daughter's cat died. It got run over... So, anyway, we buried our cat and I started to think about burials...'*

*(From an interview with Stephen King by Abe Peck, published in* Rolling Stone College Papers, *Winter 1980.)*

SCREENPLAY:
**Stephen King**; based on his own novel

Photographer: **Peter Stein**. Editors: **Michael Hill, Daniel Haley**. Production designer: **Michael Z. Hanan**. Art director: **Dins Danielsen**. Sound: **Mark Ulano, Phil Bulla**. Music: **Elliot Goldenthal**. Costume designer: **Marlene Stewart**. Make-up designer: **Hiram Ortiz**. Special make-up effects: **Lance Anderson, David Anderson**. Special visual effects: **Fantasy 2**; supervisor: **Gene Warren Jnr**. Special effects co-ordinator: **Peter M. Chesney**. Animal trainers: **Brian McMillan, Scott Hart**. **Technicolor. Dolby stereo**.

RUNNING TIME:
**103 mins**

*CHRISTINE* (1983) — and there seemed no harm in taking a breather and avoiding over-exposure. What happened next, however, was that one Stephen King movie after another appeared which did not do well at the box-office. There were exceptions, such as *STAND BY ME* (1986), but most King movies had takings that were nothing for a movie investor or distributor to become excited about.

On top of that, Stephen King wasn't behaving like a man who ought to be grateful to anyone who would film his books; he was getting much more fussy about who did what. Whoever undertook *PET SEMATARY* had to agree to use his screenplay, without any significant changes, and also had to agree to shoot it in his home state of Maine. Finally, Paramount (second time around) said 'OK' — just at a moment when George Romero was up to his neck in finishing off his *MONKEY SHINES* (1988). So even though Romero had storyboarded the film and was eager to film it, another director had to be called in.

The one they found was Mary Lambert, a fan of Stephen King's ever since reading *The Shining*. Richard Rubinstein, the movie's producer, had

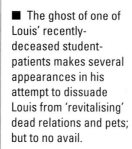

■ The ghost of one of Louis' recently-deceased student-patients makes several appearances in his attempt to dissuade Louis from 'revitalising' dead relations and pets; but to no avail.

been impressed with her work on TV commercials and pop videos (including Madonna's 'Material Girl', 'Like a Virgin' and 'Like a Prayer', Sting's 'We'll Be Together Tonight' and Janet Jackson's 'Nasty Boys'), and with her first feature, *SIESTA* (1987), an erotic, surrealistic tale of obsession. For Lambert there was a significant correlation between that film and King's book, '*Pet Sematary* is about the love of a father for his child that is obsessive to the point of breaking certain taboos, passing certain boundaries that shouldn't be passed.' Lambert tells how the first time she read King's script she was scared to death. She was alone in her own haunted house, and finished reading it in the early hours of the morning. She thought that it was a great script, but that she wouldn't possibly be able to direct it because it was 'too scary!'. She finally fell asleep, but she woke up the next morning determined to make the movie.

Every horror movie needs one or more HOB (Head On Backwards) characters — preferably whole families

■ Dr Louis Creed paying one of his midnight visits to the Micmac ground. But what is he carrying?

### KING ON PET SEMATARY

'This movie is very special to me. It's the first screenplay I've adapted from one of my novels. And it's my first book to be filmed in my home state of Maine, where many of my stories are set. What was interesting in writing the script was that there were things not in the book I realized I could add.'

'I think it does what horror movies are supposed to do. A lot of the reviews ... have suggested very strongly that people are offended by the picture, and that's exactly the effect that the horror movie seeks.

'[Mary Lambert] did a good job. She went in and she didn't flinch. In a way, that's a pretty good compliment to the way that I work... My idea is to go in there and hit as hard as you can. Mary understood that.'

(From an interview with Stephen King, by Gary Wood, Published in Cinefantastique, February 1991.)

of them. HOBs are, in reality terms, nerds. Minimum requirements are that they can be guaranteed to: shortcut through woods, or unlit lanes, after nightfall; go downstairs in the early hours to investigate strange noises; descend into cellars to discover why all the lights have gone out; open a door or window and go outside at night to search for any unknown (preferably terrifying) face seen peering in. Highly prized HOBs bury their relations in Indian burial grounds with known zombie propensities, and will move, with pets and small children, to houses adjacent to juggernaut highways whose lethal tendencies are signposted in large, misspelt letters by the 'Pet Sematary' next door.

The Creed Family are, clearly, a class act. They are so disaster-addicted that a teenage ghost, Victor Pascow, is worried enough to turn up several times to try and divert them from catastrophe — but to no avail. The Creed's 'doomy' determination has a bizarrely comic tinge. All over the world a helpless glee creeps into incredulous viewers' gasps of 'Oh wow! They really are going to be that stupid'. One of King's gifts lies in his effortless mix of the blackly macabre and the impossibly silly. For instance, Victor, throughout, never quite seems to get the hang of being 'ghoulish'; and Louis has to work out how to rip a dead cat off a frozen lawn (it makes an extraordinary sound when he does). And at one of the most terrifying moments in the film, when two-year-old Gage — now an undead child fiend who has killed Jud and his mother — is stopped by his father with a lethal injection, he pouts, 'Not fair'!

The combination of unexpected humour, gripping tension, jolting terror, unhingeing horror, genuine anguish and merciless pacing (as when little Gage and the truck are on a sure collision course) all added up to *PET SEMATARY* moving into third place on the list of all-time most successful horror movies (behind *ALIENS* (1986) and *POLTERGEIST* (1982)), and, thereafter, to Stephen King's name remaining firmly above his movie titles.

### PET SEMATARY II

*PET SEMATARY* was so successful that it was bound to spawn a sequel. However, it is one that had no input from Stephen King. Mary Lambert directed once again, this time the screenplay was by Richard Outten, and it was produced by Ralph S. Singleton (who directed and co-produced *GRAVEYARD SHIFT* (1990)). It tells the story of Chase Matthews (played by Anthony Edwards), a veterinary surgeon who moves with his son Jeff (Edward Furlong) to Ludlow, Maine, in order to help Jeff recover from his mother's death. Jeff makes friends with Gus (Clancy Brown), and when Gus's beloved dog is killed by his sadistic stepfather, the boys bury it in the Indian burial ground — and so the cycle begins again...

■ Two-year-old Gage goes on a murderous rampage after returning from the grave. It was out of the question for little Miko Hughes to play those scenes, so a cast of his head was taken and an articulated puppet created that 'stood in' for him in the more grisly episodes.

**The Films of Stephen King**

DIRECTOR:
**John Harrison**
*(USA, 1990)*

LEADING PLAYERS:
*WRAP-AROUND STORY:*
**Deborah Harry** (Betty),
**David Forrester** (priest),
**Matthew Lawrence**
(Timmy).
*LOT 246:*
**Christian Slater** (Andy),
**Robert Sedgwick** (Lee),
**Steve Buscemi** (Edward
Bellingham), **Donald Van
Horn** (removals man),
**Michael Deak** (mummy),
**Julianne Moore** (Susan),
**George Guidall** (museum
director), **Kathleen Chalfant**
(the Dean), **Ralph Marrero**
(cabbie).
*CAT FROM HELL:*
**David Johansen** (Halston),
**Paul Greene** (cabbie),
**William Hickey** (Drogan),
**Alice Drummond** (Carolyn),
**Delores Sutton** (Amanda),
**Mark Margolis** (Gage).
*LOVER'S VOW:*
**James Remar** (Preston),
**Ashton Wise** (Jer), **Philip
Lenkowsky** (Maddox),
**Robert Klein** (Wyatt), **Rae
Dawn Chong** (Carola), **Joe
Dabenigno, Larry Silvestri**
(policemen), **Donna Davidge**
(gallery patron), **Nicole
Leach** (Margaret), **Daniel
Harrison** (John), **Joel
Valentine** (gargoyle voice).

PRODUCTION COMPANY:
**Paramount**

PRODUCERS:
**Richard P. Rubinstein,
Mitchell Galin**

CO-PRODUCER:
**David Kappes**

SCREENPLAY:
**Michael McDowell:** *LOT 249*
(based on a story by **Arthur
Conan Doyle**), *WRAP-
AROUND STORY, LOVER'S
VOW.* **George Romero:** *CAT
FROM HELL,* based on a
story by **Stephen King**.

# Tales from the Darkside 1990

*Timmy's in trouble.
Will the Cat from Hell
spare him a life?*

## SYNOPSIS

**W**RAP-AROUND STORY:
Betty is preparing for
a dinner-party. Little
Timmy is the 'meat'
course and he attempts
to delay his dreadful fate
by telling Betty some
horror stories.

**LOT 249:** Vengeful
Edward Bellingham, a graduate
student, collects antiques. In 'Lot
249' is a 3000-year-old coffin
containing a mummy. Edward
manages to revive it and sends it
after two fellow students who
cheated him of a scholarship, but
their mummified remains also want
vengeance...

**CAT FROM HELL:** Drogan, a paraplegic millionaire, hires Halston to
kill the stray cat that has killed
several people close to him. Drogan
is certain he's next on the cat's hitlist because he used thousands of
cats in laboratory tests for the drug
that made him his fortune. Halston
spends a terrifying night with the
cat. It finally crawls through his
mouth to his stomach. Drogan dies
of a heart attack when the cat reappears through Halston's face.

**LOVER'S VOW:** Preston witnesses
a gruesome murder by a demon
who spares his life on condition
that he tells no one. On the way
home, Preston meets, and later
marries, Carola, the 'perfect' lady.
Ten years later, on their anniversary, he tells her his secret, only to
learn that she is the monster...

**WRAP-AROUND STORY:** Betty
wants *no* more stories. It's time to
roast Timmy. However, he trips her
up and pushes her into the oven...

**W**ith the success of *PET SEMATARY*
signalling a new surge of interest in
Stephen King movies, Richard
Rubinstein of Laurel Entertainment
began looking for another such
project. Rubinstein had for some time
been producing the TV series *TALES
FROM THE DARKSIDE.* Over the years
he had acquired stories for the series
which, for various reasons, proved

unsuitable for TV transmission.
Nevertheless, Rubinstein felt some of
them were excellent tales — including
one called 'Cat From Hell' by Stephen
King, for which George Romero had
written a script.

Rubinstein had also produced
*CREEPSHOW* (1982) and *CREEPSHOW
2* (1987) so he had plenty of experience of the horror-compendium

movie. Laurel decided to go ahead with *TALES OF THE DARKSIDE: THE MOVIE*, blending three of the 'left-over' tales with a wrap-around story. John Harrison was invited to direct the movie; he had already written a number of episodes of the TV series and directed others. Harrison had, in addition, composed the soundtrack for George Romero's *CREEPSHOW* (1982), so he was familiar with many aspects of the film side of the Stephen King phenomenon.

Michael McDowell's screenplay for the *WRAP-AROUND STORY* was a charming update of *Hansel and Gretel*. Deborah Harry plays the glamorous Betty, preparing one of her sought-after dinner parties in her elegant kitchen — except for the dark, dank dungeon of a larder wherein she is fattening up little Timmy. The boy, however, isn't cowed, and converses with Betty on such subjects as how long it will take to gut him (an hour) and roast him (they decide 12 minutes per lb, at 350°F) while he works out his plan of escape. He wins some extra time when Betty hands him a book — *Tales From the Darkside* — and he is

able to distract her with its stories.

John Harrison described *CAT FROM HELL* as 'a bizarre, supernatural, dark-action piece done totally balls-out for high suspense and weirdness'. He avoided filling the episode with shots of the cat, and settled instead for filming much of Halston's scary contest with his intended victim from the cat's eye point of view.

There was a certain amount of concern as to whether cat-fanciers would be aghast at the animal's actions in killing Halston — which, needless to say, were produced simply by some first-rate special-effects work. Indeed, in King's original story, the cat had clawed and chewed its way out through Halston's stomach.

Of Laurel Entertainment's long-time association with Stephen King — even when it's only for a slice of a movie — producer Richard Rubinstein says, 'Steve's material... I consider some of the best that's available — and it's as simple as that!'

■ Betty, a charming hostess, renowned for her *cordon bleu* dinner parties, is having trouble with the meat course: little Timmy is plotting how to stay out of the oven.

Photographer: **Robert Draper**. Editor: **Harry B. Miller III**. Production designer: **Ruth Ammon**. Art director: **Jocelyne Beaudoin**. Sound: **Weldon Brown, Michael Cerone**. Music: *CAT FROM HELL* **Chaz Jankel**; other episodes **Donald A. Rubinstein, Jim Manzie, Pat Regan, John Harrison**. Costume designer: **Ida Gearon**. Make-up: **Nancy Tong**. Special make-up effects supervisors: **Robert Kurtzman, Greg Nicotero, Howard Berger**. Make-up-effects consultant: **Dick Smith**. Special-effects supervisor: **Drew Jiritano**. Stunt co-ordinator: **Edgard Mourino**. Animal trainers: **Brian McMillan, Stacy Regan**. **Technicolor. Dolby stereo.**

RUNNING TIME: **93 mins**

# Graveyard Shift

DIRECTOR:
**Ralph S. Singleton**
*(USA, 1990)*

LEADING PLAYERS:
**David Andrews** (John Hall),
**Kelly Wolf** (Jane
Wisconsky), **Stephen
Macht** (Warwick), **Andrew
Divoff** (Danson), **Vic Polizos**
(Brogan), **Brad Dourif** (The
Exterminator), **Robert Allen
Bleuth** (Ippeston), **Ilona
Margolis** (Nardello), **Jimmy
Woodard** (Charlie
Carmichael), **Jonathan
Emerson** (Jason Reed),
**Minor Rootes** (Stevenson),
**Kelly L. Goodman**
(Warwick's secretary),
**Susan Lowden** (Daisy May),
**Joe Perham** (mill inspector),
**Dana Packard, Skip
Wheeler, Richard France,
Anne Rooney, Raissa
Danilova** (millworkers),
**Emmet Kane**
(Exterminator's assistant).

PRODUCTION COMPANY:
**Graveyard Inc.**

PRODUCERS:
**William J. Dunn, Ralph S.
Singleton.**

SCREENPLAY:
**John Esposito**; based on
the short story by **Stephen
King**, from his *Night Shift*
collection.

Photographer: **Peter Stein**.
Editors: **Jim Gross, Randy
Jon Morgan**. Production
designer: **Gary Wissner**. Art
director; **Jack Jennings.**
Sound: **Bernie Blynder**.
Music: **Anthony Marinelli,
Brian Banks**. Costume
design: **Sarah Lemire**. Key
make-up: **Jane Brickman**.
Special-effects supervisor:
**Peter M. Chesney**. Visual
consultant: **Harold
Michelson**. Visual-effects
advisor: **Albert Whitlock**.
Creature-effects supervi-
sor: **Gordon J. Smith.**

## 1983

### *Being afraid of the dark is the least of their fears*

### SYNOPSIS

**D**rifter Jon Hall arrives in Gates Falls, Maine, and gets a job at the Bachman (textile) Mills. The mills are overrun with huge rats with a taste for human flesh — having long lunched at the cemetery next door. The mill is under a closure order, following the suspicious death in the basement of a mill worker, but this has been suppressed by the mill's foreman, Warwick. Another worker dies, Warwick's secretary has a fatal 'accident' after discovering the mill-closure papers, and a rat extermina-tor also comes to a gruesome end.

Anyone querying Warwick's working practices — including Hall and Jane Wisconsky (who rejected Warwick's advances and is getting friendly with Hall) — is sent to work in the rat-infested basement. Warwick offers the basement team double pay to work over the 4th of July holiday. On the next shift, Hall uncovers a trapdoor, leading to a myriad of caves and passages. Another of the team, Brogan, finds a severed arm, but shortly afterwards falls into a pool of water — in which something monstrous devours him.

Jane and Hall have just discovered an undergound pit cavern filled with skeletons when Warwick appears and jealously stabs Jane, but is himself then overcome by the monster. Hall makes his way up into the mill and turns on the fibre-shred-ding machine. The monster — a huge bat-winged rat — is caught by the tail and lacerated to a bloody pulp.

*G*RAVEYARD SHIFT was the 19th major film or TV adaptation of a work by Stephen King: 'his 19th nervous break-down' proclaimed one critic, despair-ingly. However, of the King films clearly not acclaimed as movie master-pieces, *GRAVEYARD SHIFT* did find a goodly number of reviewers liking it in spite of themselves.

Making a seat-gripping, rat-mutating monster is not the easiest of assign-ments. Gordon J. Smith's FXSmith company pulled out all the stops and devised a rare sonic rat, or legless bat, depending on where you were when it hit you. Director Ralph S. Singleton built up the suspense in the early part of the film by inter-cutting frequent terrifying close-ups of real rats — all of which had been superbly trained by animal wrangler Gary Gero. Cinematographer Peter Stein assisted in making the monster mysterious by pitching the lighting in the cellar at a *cinéma-vérité* level of gloom.

Stephen Macht is severely sinister as the tyrannical Warwick, David Andrews suitably cool and stoic as the new boy on the shift, and Brad Dourif is his own patented brand of bizarre as Tucker Cleveland, the rat-catcher. Dourif described his character as 'the cheapest terminator around; he'll travel anywhere and always underbids his competition because he loves his work so much.' Cleveland has grisly tales to tell of fighting man-eating rats in Vietnam. There are two women, but one, Kelly L. Goodman as Warwick's beleaguered secretary, is killed off early on, and the other, Kelly Wolf as a millworker — well, what with the dark and the dirt, it's hard to tell.

King offered his story to William J. Dunn, a fellow Maine resident, who had been in charge of finding locations for *CREEPSHOW 2* (1987) and *PET SEMATARY* (1989) — both also filmed in Maine. *GRAVEYARD SHIFT*, however, was the first film in which an attempt was made to use Maine dialect: yes, that's the accent that Stephen Macht is using; no, he's not playing an Afrikaaner.

Stephen King's 'Graveyard Shift', which runs to 20 pages in the paperback edition of his *Night Shift* anthology, was, as is par for the course, considerably gloomier than the film version. For a start, there was not a trace of any female element, not even a short-lived woman.

Nor was there the tiniest glimmer of a happy ending. In the story, it's not the mutated rat-bat's tail that gets caught in the shredder, it's Jon Hall's neck that it whips its tail around and squeezes, while sinking in its teeth. The real rats then join in the fun, and, after a tasty snack, they all settle back to wait for the next shift to come back down into the cellar...

Special vocal effects: **Frank Welker**. Stunt co-ordinator: **Randy 'Fife'**. Sound-effects: **Jon Johnson**. Animal wrangler: **Gary Gero**. Colour: **DeLuxe**; prints by **Technicolor. Dolby stereo**.

RUNNING TIME: **87 minutes**

■ Warwick, the brutish foreman of the Bachman Mills, is responsible for the graveyard shift. Anyone who doesn't submit to his bullying runs the risk of being consigned to the basement rats.

DIRECTOR:
**Rob Reiner**
*(USA, 1990)*

LEADING PLAYERS:
**James Caan** (Paul Sheldon), **Kathy Bates** (Annie Wilkes), **Richard Farnsworth** (Sheriff Buster), **Frances Sternhagen** (Virginia), **Lauren Bacall** (Marcia Sindell), **Graham Jarvis** (Libby), **Jerry Potter** (Pete), **Tom Brunelle** (anchorman), **June Christopher** (anchor-woman), **Julie Payne**, **Archie Hahn III**, **Gregory Snegoff** (reporters), **Wendy Bowers** (waitress).

PRODUCTION COMPANY:
**Castle Rock Entertainment**

PRODUCERS:
**Andrew Scheinman, Rob Reiner**

CO-PRODUCERS:
**Jeffrey Scott, Steve Nicolaides**

SCREENPLAY:
**William Golding**; based on the novel by **Stephen King**

Photographer: **Barry Sonnenfeld**. Editor: **Robert Leighteon**. Production designer: **Norman Garwood**. Art director: **Mark Mansbridge**. Sound: **Robert Eber, Mark 'Frito' Long**. Music: **Marc Shaiman**. Costume designer: **Gloria Gresham**. Make-up: **John Elliott, Margaret Elliott**. Special make-up effects: **KNB EFX Group**. Special effects supervisor: **Phil Corey**. Stunt co-ordinator: **David Ellis**. Colour: **CFI**.

RUNNING TIME:
**107 mins**

# Misery

## 1990

*If he was Bad and Didn't Do What Nurse Told Him, she would be cross — very cross — and do things that would make him scream and scream ...*

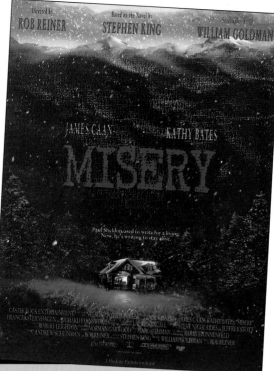

## SYNOPSIS

**P**aul Sheldon, the author of a series of best-sellers about Misery Chastain, a fictional 19th Century romantic heroine, has completed a new 'gritty' story based on his own tough childhood. He is driving back from his Colorado mountain hideaway home through severe blizzards when his car swerves into a ravine. He is rescued by Annie Wilkes, who declares herself to be his 'Number One Fan'. Paul's legs are broken, but, being a former nurse, she is able to splint them. However, on reading his new novel, Annie is angered by the 'profane' language it contains and forces him to burn it. When she acquires a copy of his latest 'Misery' book, *Misery's Child*, she is further enraged to find that Misery dies in childbirth. She keeps Paul impris-

oned while he writes a new book resurrecting 'Misery' — when he tries to escape she breaks his ankles.

Meanwhile, Paul's agent, Marcia Sindell, is worried about his disappearance. She alerts a local sheriff who finally tracks Paul down to Annie's house, but she shoots him before he can raise the alarm.

Paul does complete the new Misery novel but, during the celebration dinner Annie prepares, he burns the manuscript before her eyes. She shoots him, but he manages to knock her out with his typewriter and then kill her.

After he is rescued and has recovered, his new-style novel is warmly acclaimed by the critics, but a disapproving Annie Wilkes haunts his waking nightmares.

**S**tephen King wasn't keen to sell the movie rights to *Misery*; it was a novel that was much too personal for him. Finally, however, he agreed to sell them to Castle Rock Entertainment on condition that one of its partners — Rob Reiner — be closely associated with the film. Reiner, of course, had already directed one of King's favourite 'King' movies — *STAND BY ME* (1986), and, although the author

said he would feel '*fairly* comfortable' if Reiner merely masterminded the film's production, he did hope that Reiner would choose to direct it himself, 'That's what I had my fingers crossed for the whole time.'

Initially, Reiner was only interested in Castle Rock producing the film, but then he read what he considered was a very good screenplay by William Golding. He found himself becoming really intrigued by the movie's subject matter, and finally decided that he would direct proceedings himself. Not a small part of the decision was because his friend Stephen King cared so deeply about this book, 'He didn't want to see it destroyed'.

There were several clear parallels between the circumstances of Stephen King and Paul Sheldon. In terms of Sheldon's wish to give up writing 'Misery' pulp fiction and turn to 'serious' writing, Reiner could see how King might be equally tormented, 'He is wondering, "Can I write something other than the kinds of things I've been writing? Will I lose my audience?" That's what fascinated me.'

Then there was the paradoxically aligned but opposing issue of the rights of that audience. An author who spends most of his time on the best-seller lists has made a pact with his readers: they buy his books in huge quantities, thereby providing him with a large income. However, the bargain is that he continues to be their best-selling author, producing the juice they know and love, and that he doesn't say, 'Thank you, I've got enough money now, so I shall live off it while I write "prose"'. 'Oh no, you won't,' say the Annie Wilkeses. 'You're ours; you'll do as you're told!'

Stephen King tells a scary story which was part of his reason for writing *Misery*. A fan asked King to pose with him for a polaroid photo. He then produced a 'special pen' and asked King to sign the photo 'Best wishes to Mark Chapman from Stephen King', telling him that he was

■ Annie Wilkes is a nurse in a million. She'll save your life, and nurse you back to health, and then she'll cripple you all over again.

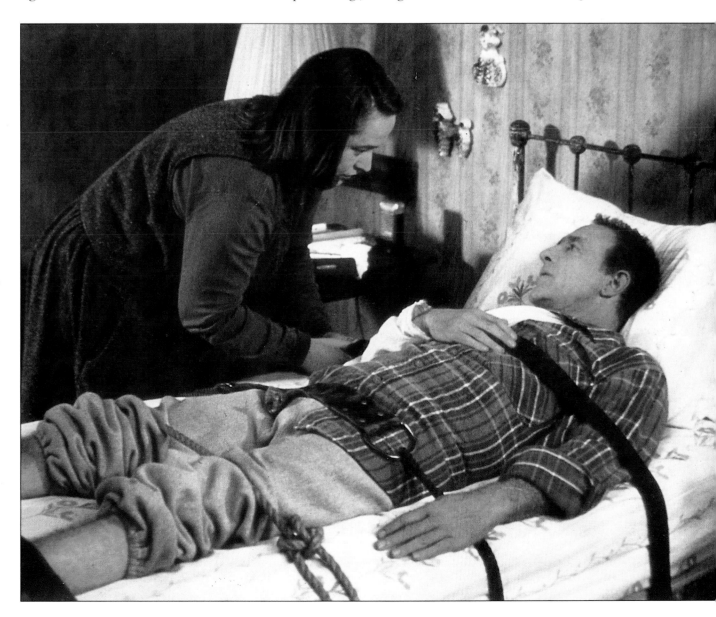

■ Nurse Wilkes pops down to the cellar to check on her patient. The hypodermic, through which she's keeping Paul pain-killer dependent, is as big a threat as the gun.

King's 'Number One Fan'. Mark Chapman was the young man who killed John Lennon — an hour or so after getting Lennon's autograph.

The first job for screenwriter William Golding (Oscar-winner for *BUTCH CASSIDY AND THE SUNDANCE KID* (1969), and *ALL THE PRESIDENT'S MEN* (1976)) was to open up King's storyboard. The plot of *Misery*, with the exception of the last 10 pages, takes place in Annie Wilkes's home.

Golding initially thought of dipping in and out of the Misery Chastain stories, as King does, but decided he didn't have the gift for 'True Romance' tales. Instead, he opted for expanding the role of Sheriff Buster, who only appears at the very end of the book. In the film, Buster is alerted by literary agent Marcia Sindell who is worried by Sheldon's disappearance. The tight drama of the increasingly obsessed, moody and violent fan, and the

## THE ODD COUPLE

**KATHY BATES**

'I wrote the part [of Annie Wilkes] for Kathy,' said William Golding. 'I'd never met her, but when I read King's book I thought, "Kathy Bates would be great for this part". She's one of our leading actresses but, because she's not a "conventional beauty", most of the film stuff she's done has been left on the cutting-room floor, or it's just been little parts.' Indeed, the most notable thing about Bates's movie career till then had been the roles she hadn't played. She had major theatre successes in *Night Mother* — her role was played on screen by Sissy Spacek; *Crimes of the Heart* — played in the film by Diane Keaton; and as a dowdy waitress in *Frankie and Johnny in the Clair de Lune* — which went to Michelle Pfeiffer.

But at the Academy Awards ceremony in March 1991, the biggest roar of the night went up for Kathy Bates's Best Actress Oscar for her performance in *MISERY*.

(From an interview with William Golding, by Nigel Floyd, published in *Time Out*, 7 May 1991.)

**JAMES CAAN**

The tables were turned on James Caan for his role as Paul Sheldon in *MISERY*, because his first 'proper' movie role was in *LADY IN A CAGE* (1964), when he played the part of one of three youths who keep a rich widow imprisoned in the elevator of her mansion house while they taunt her and ransack her home.

Rob Reiner had worked quite extensively on the role of Paul Sheldon with Warren Beatty, but Beatty had decided to pull out in order to concentrate on his *DICK TRACY* (1990). 'I went through a number of actors [Michael Douglas, Harrison Ford, William Hurt, Robert Redford, Richard Dreyfuss and Dustin Hoffman] before Jimmy,' Reiner recalls.

'But looking back on it, I can't imagine anyone other than Jimmy doing it. He's so good in it.' So why did Caan accept the role? 'I think,' said Reiner, 'he wanted the work.'

(From an interview with Rob Reiner, by Alan Jones, published in *Empire* magazine, April 1991.)

## REINER ON KING

'Stephen King says *MISERY* is his most favourite film ever made from one of his books. He gave me a big hug after the first screening in Los Angeles and I was thrilled with his reaction.

'King is a good writer, he pens wonderfully complex characters and great dialogue ... Yet when people adapt his books into movies they tend to ... just concentrate on the Horror and the Supernatural — all the things that seem to be the most overtly commercial. It's a grave mistake because they lose many levels of his work by doing the obvious.'

(From an interview with Rob Reiner, by Alan Jones, published in *Starburst* magazine, April 1991.)

unbearably frustrated, frightened and pain-ridden writer is inter-cut with some comic-relief episodes involving super-sleuth Buster and his disapproving wife Virginia. These additional scenes, Golding felt, didn't alter the central focus of the novel in any way, but did allow the audience occasionally to 'get out of the house'.

Another much-discussed departure from the novel concerned the 'hobbling' of Sheldon. In the novel, after discovering that he's been trying to escape, Annie Wilkes chops off one of his legs with an axe, and then cauterizes the 'stump' with a blowtorch. Reiner felt that the film's audience would never forgive Annie, and settled instead for breaking Sheldon's ankles. It was, nevertheless, a very graphic scene, thanks to excellent gelatin legs provided by the KNB EFX Group. They also created the 'Sheldon arm' into which Wilkes injects addictive painkillers, one of her 'Misery'-writing inducements.

The end of the film also differed from the book. In the novel, Sheldon didn't burn *Misery's Return*, and, once he had made his escape, he published it, accepting that his job was to go on writing 'Misery' novels. Reiner felt that, 'If he does that, he's the same guy coming out that he was going in. And I think if there's any growth in the character, that's what it ought to be.'

**The Films of Stephen King**

# Sleepwalkers 1992

*If Charles invites you round for lunch, don't go. You're it!*

DIRECTOR:
**Mick Garris**
*(USA, 1992)*

LEADING PLAYERS:
**Brian Krause** (Charles Brady), **Mädchen Amick** (Tanya Robertson), **Alice Krige** (Mary Brady), **Jim Haynie** (Sheriff Ira), **Cindy Pickett** (Mrs Robertson), **Ron Perlman** (Captain Soames), **Lyman Ward** (Don Robertson), **Dan Martin** (Andy Simpson), **Glenn Shadix** (Mr Fallows), **Cynthia Garris** (Laurie), **Monty Bane** (Horace), **John Landis** (lab technician), **Joe Dante** (lab assistant), **Stephen King** (cemetery caretaker), **Clive Barker, Tobe Hooper** (forensic technicians), **O. Nicholas Brown** (Officer Wilbur), **Mark Hamill.**

PRODUCTION COMPANY:
**Columbia Pictures**

PRODUCERS:
**Mark Victor, Michael Grais, Nabeel Zahid**

CO-PRODUCER:
**Richard Stenta**

SCREENPLAY:
**Stephen King**

Photographer: **Rodney Charters**. Editor: **O. Nicholas Brown**. Production designer: **John DeCuir Jnr**. Art director: **Sig Tinglof**. Sound: **Don H. Matthews**. Music: **Nicholas Pike**. Key make-up artists: **John Blake, Rick Stratton**. Special make-up effects: **Alterian Studios** (supervisor, **Tony Gardner**; creature-suit design/sculpture, **Tom Hester**). Special visual effects: **Apogee Productions** (supervisor, **Jeffrey A. Okun**). Stunt co-ordinator: **Phil Adams**. Animal trainers: **Terri Knapp, Sam Coulter**. Technicolor. **Dolby stereo**.

RUNNING TIME:
**91 mins**

## SYNOPSIS

Charles Brady and his mother, Mary, have come to hide out in Travis, Indiana. They are constantly on the run because they are Sleepwalkers — part-reptile, part-human and part-feline; indeed domestic cats are their greatest enemies. They are shape-shifters, and can also make themselves invisible. Male Sleepwalkers feed off the virtue of young virgins — through having sex with them and drinking their blood — and then pass this nourishment on to the female Sleepwalkers, by having sex with them. As Charles and Mary are probably all that remain of the species, their relationship is necessarily incestuous.

Charles enlists in school, and beautiful young Tanya immediately falls for him. However, when he tries to make love to her, he shape-shifts into his bestial form and she fights him off. Deputy Sheriff Simpson arrives, and is killed by Charles (who has already killed his suspicious schoolteacher), but Simpson's plucky cat Clovis wounds Charles severely. Charles goes home to his mother, who kidnaps Tanya to feed her son.

Cats are gathering on the lawn outside the house. Sheriff Ira arrives with Clovis, and Charles dies in the battle that ensues. The cats, led by Clovis, then turn on Mary, who bursts into flames. Tanya hugs Clovis, the hero of the day.

**I**n this, the first script expressly written for the screen by Stephen King, the horrormeister felt it was time we met — Sleepwalkers. As it was, he left it a bit late in the day, because it seems there were only two of them left, and those were mother and son. Moreover, they were dead by the end of the film — but, of course, in horror-film terms that's of no consequence.

'*SLEEPWALKERS,*' director Mick Garris informs us (as does the film's opening reference to the *Chillicoathe Encyclopedia of Arcane Knowledge*), 'share some genetic information with cats, as they do with humans, but they've conquered the human power. What they have not conquered is their genetic relationship with felines, and they [cats] are the only thing that can cause the Sleepwalkers fatal harm.'

But, please sir, where have these beautifully horrible creatures been all our lives? Why has no one ever reported seeing one before? Charles and Mary weren't too tidy about remaining hidden. And where did the species come from? And why are these two the last of the line?

However, we shouldn't complain. We have been given a value-for-money creature here. It's got a bit of everything. It does a human/creature, were-wolf-style shape-shift. It is unquestion-ably vampire-related. Its lizardy, reptil-ian mode could be a dragon link, or some demon-serpent (possibly prehis-toric?). It can make itself invisible — surprisingly few monsters are able to do that! It has great (though 'uncon-quered') feline interlinkings, and the cat is one of the most powerfully mysterious of animals. And at the end there was a touch of the phoenix, as Mary went up in flames. All this, and they're almost out of stock!

There was, apparently, some trouble on set convincing the cats that Sleepwalkers were their mortal enemies. They were profoundly unin-terested in Sleepwalkers — even Sleepwalkers smeared with cat food.

The incestuous nature of Sleepwalker survival was another interesting idea. Maybe — Stephen King clearly being a man of sound family values — that was why they had to go. Director Mick Garris speaks of

an early scene in which mother and son perform a slow dance together, moving steadily closer and closer to one another. 'Every time I see this scene with an audience,' says Garris, 'everyone lets out an almighty "Eeeewwww" when they kiss and Charles says, "Oh, mother".'

Another interesting element in *SLEEPWALKERS* was morphing, a computer technique that was used to transform Mary and Charles into their various Sleepwalker forms. Morphing allowed this process to happen extremely subtly. At one time, for instance, when Mary suddenly becomes quite angry, it was possible — through computer morphing — to half-shape-shift her for a few seconds.

Extra money's worth came in the form of 'spot your favourite horror-film director'. John Landis, Joe Dante, Clive Barker, Stephen King and Tobe Hooper are all in there, plus Mark Hamill and the film's editor, O. Nicholas Brown.

■ Sleepwalker Charles's last moments on earth. Tanya has forcibly resisted his efforts to make a meal of her, and plucky cat Clovis has done the rest of the damage.

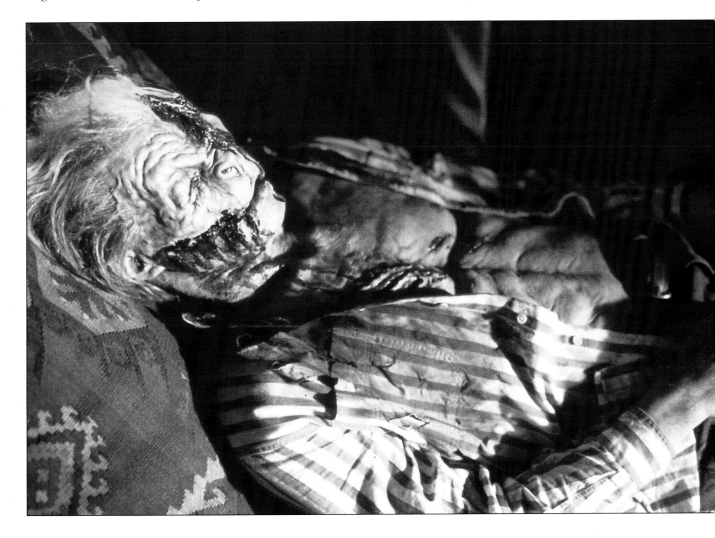

# The Dark Half

DIRECTOR:
**George A. Romero**
*(USA, released 1993;
filmed 1990-91)*

LEADING PLAYERS:
**Timothy Hutton** (Thad
Beaumont/ George Stark),
**Amy Madigan** (Liz
Beaumont), **Michael
Rooker** (Sheriff Alan
Pangborn), **Julie Harris**
(Reggie DeLesseps), **Robert
Joy** (Fred Clawson), **Kent
Broadhurst** (Mike
Donaldson), **Beth Grant**
(Shayla Beaumont),
**Rutyana Alda** (Miriam
Cowley), **Tom Madirosian**
(Rick Cowley), **Larry John
Meyers** (Dr Pritchard),
**Patrick Brannen** (young
Thad Beaumont), **Royal
Dano** (Digger Holt), **Glenn
Colerider** (Homer
Gamache), **Sarah and
Elizabeth Parker** (Wendy
and William Beaumont),
**John Ponzio** (Todd
Pangborn), **Chelsea Field**
(Annie Pangborn), **William
Cameron** (Officer Hamilton).

PRODUCTION COMPANY:
**Dark Half Productions/
Orion Pictures**

PRODUCER:
**Declan Baldwin**

SCREENPLAY:
**George A. Romero**;
based on the novel by
**Stephen King**.

Photographer: **Tony Pierce-
Roberts**. Editor: **Pasquale
Buba**. Production designer:
**Cletus Anderson**.
Art director: **Jim Feng**.
Sound: **John Sutton**.
Music: **Christopher Young**.
Costume designer: **Barbara
Anderson**. Make-up effects
created by: **John Vulich,
Everett Burrell** (Optic Nerve
F/X). Visual effects:
**VCE/Peter Kuran**.
Special-effects supervisor:
**Carl Horner Jnr**.

## 1993

*George Stark
1985-1991
Not a very nice guy*

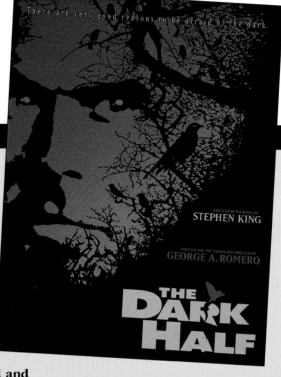

### SYNOPSIS

Whenever young Thad Beaumont starts to write a story, he gets a violent headache and hears strange noises — like hundreds of small birds screeching. One day, he blacks out from the pain. An exploratory operation reveals a bizarre growth in Thad's brain, complete with an eye, teeth and fingernails. It is Thad's twin embryo which never developed and which Thad's foetus absorbed. The growth is removed.

Thad grows up to be a writer of serious fiction, and a teacher of creative writing at a college in Maine. However, he also writes violent best-selling thrillers under the pseudonym 'George Stark'. When his alias is discovered by a blackmailer, Thad and his wife Liz decide to 'come clean' about Thad's dual identity, and then ceremoniously 'bury' George Stark in the local cemetery. A few days later a large hole is found at the graveside; something has dug its way out.

One by one, people who knew about Thad's alias are savagely slaughtered, and each time the evidence points to Thad. His headaches and blackouts return, and, after one, he sees he has written the words 'The Sparrows Are Flying Again' — words which were discovered at the scene of one of the murders. Thad finally realises that George Stark, his 'dark half', has somehow become embodied and is taking revenge for having been ceremoniously 'killed off'.

Stark, who is slowly decomposing, insists that Thad resume writing 'Stark' thrillers. He abducts Liz and the twins to the Beaumont's summer house. Thad allows his 'dark half' to begin writing again, but, just in time, the sparrows come to collect George Stark...

**S**tephen King has long been curious about the business of being a writer — both the causes and the effects. He has explored both; he has switched them round; he has doubled back and come at them from a different angle; he has slid into the twilight zone that lies between the two; he has played with the reality of the situation and its unreality; he has mixed them up; he has done it all over again, but in a different order. He said, after 'Secret Window, Secret Garden', in the *Four Past Midnight* collection (a story ostensibly about an author accused of stealing someone else's story; in fact he *had* stolen someone's story, but not *that* story), that he thought it would be his last story about writers and writing. This remains to be seen.

Before that, there had been *Misery* and *The Dark Half*. In *Misery*, a fan is murderously affronted when an author kills off her pulp-fiction heroine. In *The Dark Half*, it is an author's thriller-writing alias who is enraged at being axed when his 'better half', having got all he needs from the partnership, wishes to move on to finer things.

'*The Dark Half* is a "Jekyll and Hyde" story,' says writer-director George A. Romero, 'in the sense that it explores the dark side of all of us. It's a very thought-provoking story, because revealing our dark half not only affects our own lives but our families and relationships as well.' Romero has known Stephen King for many years. King played a beer-guzzling spectator in *KNIGHTRIDERS* (1981), Romero's movie about a travelling troupe that staged medieval fairs in which knights jousted on motorcycles, and then Romero directed King's stories/screenplay in *CREEPSHOW* (1982) and he had adapted a King story for the sequel *CREEPSHOW 2* (1987).

Romero had been actively involved in the development of *THE STAND* (due for release in 1994), *PET SEMATARY* (1989) and *IT* (1990), but for one reason or another he was unable to follow through and direct them when they finally got off the ground. He had been interested in *THE DARK HALF* from the beginning and began filming it in October 1990. The film was ready to roll the following year, but at that time one of its major backers, Orion Pictures, became embroiled in severe 'cash flow' problems. As a result, the movie was consigned to a shelf until 1993, when Orion's financial situation cheered up.

Timothy Hutton played both 'halves' of *THE DARK HALF*. Location reports say Hutton took each role equally seriously, requiring separate trailers for

Special-effects consultant: **Ed Fountain**. Stunt co-ordinator: **Phil Nielson**. Bird co-ordinator: **Mark Harden**. Colour: **DeLuxe**. **Dolby A. Stereo**.

RUNNING TIME: **124 mins**

■ The meeting that has to happen, between Thad Beaumont and George Stark, the embodiment of Thad's 'dark side'. Thad stalls for time, discussing with his alter ego the violent thriller that George Stark wants written in his (Stark's) name.

## NASTY BOYS

Creating the lean, mean look of George Stark was the job of make-up effects team John Vulich and Everett Burrell. Vulich felt 'the overall effect was to make Stark the sort of fantasy macho figure a reclusive writer like Beaumont would fantasize being ...the Marlboro man with an evil twist.' Timothy Hutton felt strongly, Burrell recalls, that Stark had to be so gross as to repulse Liz Beaumont in their scenes together, but 'he had to keep his attractiveness (to exert a subtle sexual pull). If he were too gross, people wouldn't be able to stare at him for very long. And if we went overboard, the character's feelings wouldn't "play" through the make-up.'

For the sessions when Hutton's 'Stark' make-up was applied, Vulich and Burrell created what they called a Method Make-up Trailer. In order to help Hutton get in the mood, they kept *heavy* heavy-metal music going full-blast, littered the place with empty beer and coke cans, and threw pizzas at the walls for that extra live-action touch.

(From an interview with Everett Burrell, by Charles Leayman, published in *Cinefantastique*, June 1993.)

■ *Above*: The words in blood on the wall at the scene of a murder is the final clue, for Thad, that these murders are connected with him. Through his manifested writing pseudonym, 'George Stark', he is responsible for them.

■ *Right*: George Stark kidnaps Thad's twin toddlers as a way of forcing a meeting with his better half.

Stark days and Beaumont days. He also, they say, had separate hotel rooms for the nights before Stark days and Beaumont days.

The supernatural forces in *THE DARK HALF* are represented by huge throngs of sparrows. Beaumont first hears them before the onset of his childhood headaches. Later on they arrive whenever Stark is about to put in an appearance. For these significant moments in the film, 4500 Cut Throat Finches (named for the red band around their necks) were hired. The birds ate over 100lbs of bird seed each day. They also had to have daily flying exercise in a specially constructed wind tunnel to keep them 'in shape', otherwise, bird-wrangler Mark Harden explained, they wouldn't have responded to any kind of persuasion on filming days.

Thad Beaumont learns from Reggie DeLesseps, a fellow lecturer at Ludlow college, that sparrows were considered by the ancient Greeks to be 'psychopomps' — conductors of souls between the land of the living and the kingdom of the dead. In King's novel, and in the original script, Thad's eccentric colleague and friend was a man — Rawlie DeLesseps. When it came to casting the film, the part was offered to Julie Harris (first seen on screen as the 12-year-old Frankie in *THE MEMBER OF THE WEDDING* (1952)). The role of Reggie, however, remained virtually unchanged. Rawlie smoked a briar pipe in the novel; Julie Harris puffed at one on screen.

The name 'Stark' goes back to Stephen King's childhood. He was enthralled by the late-1950s serial killer Charles Starkweather, filling a scrapbook with newspaper clippings about him. He told critic Douglas E. Winter, 'It was a young boy's first glimpse of the face of evil. I loved that guy. I thought that he was "cool as a moose", as we used to say; but at the same time, he scared me shitless. My mother was ready to have me placed in analysis.'

King has a more benign parallel to George Stark in his own life; between 1977 and 1984 he wrote five novels under the pseudonym of 'Richard

Bachman', to give himself time off from being 'Stephen King'. He, too, 'came clean' to the press after a fan discovered his dual identity, and abandoned his pseudonym. Nevertheless, his 'Author's Note' in *The Dark Half* states, 'I'm indebted to the late Richard Bachman for his help and inspiration. This novel could not have been written without him.'

■ In this splendid piece of special-effects work, Hutton is replaced by a fully mechanized puppet, wearing a 'Bird Suit'. When plugged in, the suit would deliver a frenzied attack on him.

**ROMERO ON THE DARK HALF**

'I had always wanted to adapt one of Stephen's novels. I enjoyed the challenge, because it's always difficult to compress an ambitious book into a manageable script. And because I know him so well, I was especially concerned to make sure that Stephen's voice as a writer could still be heard in the movie.'

# Needful Things

DIRECTOR:
**Fraser Heston**
*(USA, 1993)*

LEADING PLAYERS:
**Max Von Sydow** (Leland Gaunt), **Ed Harris** (Sheriff Alan Pangborn), **Bonnie Bedelia** (Polly Chalmers), **Amanda Plummer** (Nettie Cobb), **J.T. Walsh** (Danforth Keeton III), **Valri Bromfield** (Wilma Jerzyck), **Ray McKinnon** (Deputy Norris Ridgewick), **Duncan Fraser** (Hugh Priest), **W. Morgan Sheppard** (Father Meehan), **Shane Meier** (Brian Rusk).

PRODUCTION COMPANY:
**Castle Rock Entertainment**

EXECUTIVE PRODUCER:
**Peter Yates**

PRODUCER:
**Jack Cummins**

SCREENPLAY:
**W.D. Richter**; based on the novel by **Stephen King**.

Photographer: **Tony Westman**. Production designer: **Doug Higgins**. Art director: **Sheila Haley**. Sound: **Eric Batut**. Music: **Patrick Doyle**. Costume designer: **Monique Prudhomme**. Special-effects co-ordinator: **Gary Paller**. Stunt co-ordinator/2nd unit director: **Bill Ferguson**. Colour.

RUNNING TIME:
**121 mins**

## 1993

*Everyone got what they wanted. Not many lived to tell the tale...*

■ Young Brian Rusk is the first customer at Needful Things. For him, Gaunt has a prized baseball card. But there is a catch...

### SYNOPSIS

Leland Gaunt, a newcomer, arrives in Castle Rock. He opens a shop that's called 'Needful Things' and which houses a mixture of antiques and curios. He seems very courteous and pleasant, although there is something slightly sinister about him.

The citizens of Castle Rock are delighted with the 'treasures' they find at Needful Things. Mr Gaunt seems to know everyone's secret desires — and to be able to gratify them. However, Sheriff Alan Pangborn has noticed a sudden and inexplicable outbreak of senseless violence in the town.

In exchange for each of his very inexpensively priced items, Gaunt also exacts a small favour. This involves playing a 'joke' on some other member of the community. The jokes have terrible consequences. Someone throws mud at Wilma Jerzyck's sheets; she believes it was the lonely widow Nettie Cobb; Nettie thinks Wilma has murdered her little dog and the ladies come to axe-blows. Meantime, the dog-murderer and the mud-thrower are involved in their own lethal feuds with other 'jokers'.

Sheriff Pangborn, alerted by the increasingly strange behaviour of his girlfriend, Polly Chalmers, since she bought a weird piece of jewellery from Gaunt, realizes that Needful Things is the focal point of all the trouble. Gaunt does, in fact, intend to witness the destruction of Castle Rock; half the population is now eager to kill the other half.

Pangborn decides to call out the Demon Joker himself, and on an ominous, stormy night, the final battle of malevolence begins...

**Welcome to** Castle Rock, Maine, a small but beautiful seaside town in New England. Strange things have happened in Castle Rock.

There was, for instance, a nasty run of murders by a guy they called the Castle Rock Strangler, who turned out to be Deputy Sheriff Frank Dodd. He killed himself when they caught him

(in *THE DEAD ZONE* (1983)). Then there was that rabid dog (*CUJO* (1983)); it killed a good few Castle Rock folks. And what about all that trouble out at the Beaumont place (*THE DARK HALF* (1993))? However, things were looking kinda quiet until that guy, what's his name? — Gaunt, opened up that new antique shop. Gaunt is played by Max

Von Sydow, the renowned Swedish actor who starred in many of Ingmar Bergman's brooding, introspective films. In *NEEDFUL THINGS*, although he is the personification of evil, Stephen King sent Von Sydow a note asking him not to play the role as the Devil. Von Sydow immediately understood King's request, observed director Fraser Heston (son of Charlton — and here making his first feature film): 'Instead of playing this character as a monster, Max had to play him as an intelligent and immensely well-educated person who is classy and maintains, through his cutting wit, a very dry sense of humour.

'In addition, Gaunt is enormously patient and understanding, and possesses an extensive knowledge of humankind. Consequently, he is definitely the story's most interesting character because, although we disapprove of his actions, we care about and like him. And by the film's finale, we're almost ready to see him do the same things elsewhere...

'In this story, the demon, instead of directly inflicting pain on victims, manipulates people into doing his dirty work. He nudges someone into buying a gun and shooting a person whom they dislike. So people who are essentially decent folk suddenly find themselves in the middle of a war zone...'

As Gaunt exerts his influence throughout Castle Rock, the 'personal favours' he exacts as payment for the wares in his Needful Things emporium become increasingly sinister. 'Because these acts eventually lead to murder,' said Heston, 'the scenes become more and more intense. This is something we reinforced through lighting — which gradually grew darker, moodier and more ominous — and abrupt changes in weather. When we first see Castle Rock, it's a great and peaceful place to live, where, on sunny days, young men ride around on motorcycles. Then, as things get more and more malevolent, we see rain, we hear thunder — and the film's climax takes place at night...

'*NEEDFUL THINGS*,' concludes Heston, 'like *MISERY* and other Stephen King stories, possesses elements which provide enough horror — locked within the human breast — to account for more scariness than one could ever ask for.'

But wait a minute — what's happened to Castle Rock? It looks strangely faint and fuzzy. It couldn't be fading away could it...?

■ All over Castle Rock, hatred flares up as its citizens become the victims of very nasty 'jokes'. Each is planned by Gaunt to point to someone other than the real culprit, thus setting up a knock-on stream of misplaced revenge.

# Night Shift Shorts

*THE WOMAN IN THE ROOM
(USA, 1983)*
Released by Granite
Entertainment on video as
*STEPHEN KING'S NIGHT
SHIFT COLLECTION* (1986).

DIRECTOR:
**Frank Darabont**

LEADING PLAYERS:
**Michael Cornelison** (John
Elliott), **Dee Croxton**
(Mother/Donna Elliott),
**Brian Libby** (prisoner),
**Bob Brunson** (1st guard),
**George Russell** (2nd guard).

PRODUCER:
**Gregory Melton**

SCREENPLAY:
**Frank Darabont**; based on the
story by **Stephen King** from
his *Night Shift* collection.

Photographer: **Juan Ruiz
Anchia**. Editors: **Frank
Darabont, Kevin Rock**.
Art director: **Gregory
Melton**. Location sound
mixer: **Darryl Linkow**.
Costume designer:
**Giovanna Melton**.
Make-up: **Tom Schwartz**.

RUNNING TIME:
**32 mins**

*THE BOOGEYMAN
(USA, 1983)*
Released by Granite
Entertainment on video as
*STEPHEN KING'S NIGHT
SHIFT COLLECTION* (1986).

DIRECTOR:
**Jeffrey C. Schiro**

LEADING PLAYERS:
**Michael Reid** (Lester
Billings), **Bert Linder** (Dr
Harper), **Terence Brady** (Sgt
Gurland), **Mindy Silverman**
(Rita Billings), **Jerome
Bynder** (coroner), **Bobby
Persicheth** (Denny), **Michael
Dagostino** (Andy), **Nancy
Lindeberg** (the neighbour).

PRODUCER:
**Jeffrey C. Schiro**

SCREENPLAY:
**Jeffrey C. Schiro**; based on
the story by **Stephen King**
from his *Night Shift* collection.

Photographer: **Douglas
Meltzer**. Sound design:
**Jeffrey C. Schiro, John**

## 1983-1987

*'Let's talk, you and I.
Let's talk about fear.'*

**N**ot so very long ago, when
you went to the cinema, you
saw either a double bill or a
feature plus cartoons plus a
short. Sometimes the short
was a piece of barely
disguised propaganda;
sometimes it was a travel-
ogue that moved you
around by means of
achingly bad puns; but
sometimes it turned out to
be a little gem.

Somewhere, shorts are
still shown — they get
Oscars, so they must get
seen. One Oscar-
contender was *THE
WOMAN IN THE ROOM*
(1983), directed by film-
school graduate Frank
Darabont. It tells of a
suffering mother, termi-
nally ill with cancer (as
King's own mother had
been), and the anguish
of her son who cannot
bear being unable to help her.
Darabont's script added a character: a
prisoner who is appealing against his
death sentence. His lawyer is the son,
John Elliott.

The prisoner speaks of having killed
his best friend who was dying of
gangrene in Vietnam, 'Hell, he saved
my life once. I owed him.' This helps
John make the decision to give his
mother the pills she needs to 'go to
sleep'. Nevertheless, John is still
plagued by indecision and guilt, as
Darabont shows in a powerful dream
sequence in which John's mother
pursues him through hospital corridors
in a wheelchair.

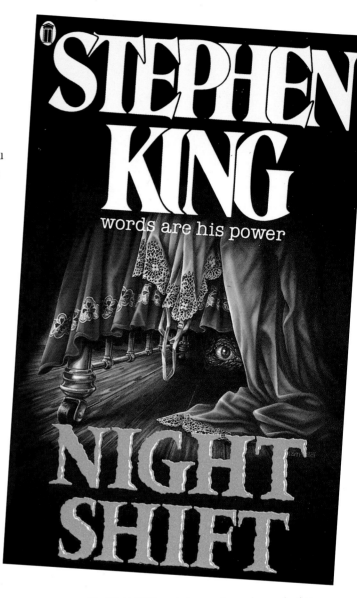

■ *Night Shift* contains such movie-producing
stories as 'Quitters Inc.' and 'The Ledge' (CAT'S
EYE (1985)), 'The Children of the Corn',
'Graveyard Shift', 'Sometimes They Come Back'
and 'The Mangler' (in pre-production in 1993).

Stephen King described *THE
WOMAN IN THE ROOM* as '... clearly
the best of the short films made from
my stuff.' The film was put onto a video
entitled 'Two Mini-Features From
Stephen King's *Night Shift* Collection'
— the other mini-feature being *THE
BOOGEYMAN* (1983). Jeff Schiro got
King's permission to film this story for
his New York University Film School
course. The Boogeyman is the terror in

the life of Lester Billings, a man whose children are mysteriously dying. Billings tells Dr Harper, a psychiatrist, that the boogeyman did it, 'He came out of the closet and killed them all.' Billings, as played by Michael Reid, is very sinister, and only at the film's end does the real villain actually materialize. Schiro won an award for *THE BOOGEYMAN* at the NYU Film Festival.

Two other stories from the *Night Shift* collection have been turned into very commendable short films. Both, again, are student projects. *THE LAST RUNG ON THE LADDER* (1987) was directed by James Cole and Dan Thron on a budget of about $1500, and was shot on Super 8mm. It is a bleak tale. Larry and his sister Kitty, when very young, sneak into a barn and dive from the loft down onto the hay-stacked floor far below.

The years pass and they become bigger and heavier until one day the ladder to the loft collapses under them. Kitty is left hanging by her fingertips, while Larry just manages in time to collect enough hay for a safe landing. They grow up and move apart. But things go wrong for Kitty, and she writes a despairing letter to Larry, who is now an attorney, but he doesn't find time to reply. She makes her last jump — from a skyscraper roof.

Producer Milton Subotsky owned the film rights to *The Lawnmower Man*, and his movie of that name (though, King claimed, not of that story) finally appeared in 1992. Meantime, Jim Gonis directed his *THE LAWNMOWER MAN* (1987). It was deemed a very professional job — and very true to the original story.

It tells of lawnmowerless Howard Parkette whose grass has become so long that he has to hire some help. The 'help' duly arrives, in the form of the grossly fat Karras who brings along with him a very old red power-mower. The lawnmower man crawls along behind the mower eating everything the mower slices up — grass, moles, etc. When Parkette complains, the lawnmower sets off after him...

*THE LAWNMOWER MAN*'s film-makers give an enthusiastic account of their 'labour of love'. A guinea pig stood in for the live mole; the dead mole was boiled liver, food colouring and a rabbit pelt; the power-mower had smoke bombs taped inside to give off the 'exhaust'. The movie was shown at the Horrorfest '89 Film festival.

■ Lester Billings is distraught — pale and trembling. The boogeyman came out of a closet and killed his children one by one.
Will Dr. Harper, his psychiatrist, believe him?

Coté. Set design: **Susan Schiro**. Location sound: **John Vittolo, Dave Smith, Kurt Hathaway**. Production assistants: **Michael Berkman, Mark Fitzmartic, Kurt Hathaway, Susan Schiro, Joe Shulder, John Walsh**.

RUNNING TIME:
**29 mins**

*THE LAST RUNG ON THE LADDER*
(USA, 1987 — unreleased)

DIRECTORS:
**James Cole, Dan Thron**

LEADING PLAYERS:
**Adam Houhoulis** (Larry), **Melissa Whelden** (Kitty), **Nat Wordell** (Father), **Adam Howes** (older Larry).

PRODUCTION COMPANY:
An independent production of **Talisman Films**

PRODUCER:
**James Cole**

SCREENPLAY:
**James Cole, Dan Thron**; based on a story in **Stephen King**'s *Night Shift* collection.

Photographer: **Dan Thron**. Editor: **James Cole**. Sound: **James Cole, Dan Thron**. Music: **Anne Livermore**.

RUNNING TIME:
**12 mins 20 secs**

*THE LAWNMOWER MAN*
(USA, 1987 - unreleased)

DIRECTOR:
**Jim Gonis**

LEADING PLAYERS:
**E.D. Phillips** (Parkette), **Andy Clark** (Karras), **Helen Hanft** (Mrs Parkette), **Tony Di Sante** (cop), **Robert Tossberg** (cop 'Bannerman'), **Neil Schimmel** (neighbour Castonmeyer), **Becky Taub** (girl), **Fayth Schlossberg** (Sheila).

PRODUCER:
**Jim Gonis**

SCREENPLAY:
**Mike De Luca**; based on the story by **Stephen King** in his *Night Shift* collection.

Photographer: **Ethan Reiff**. Editor: **Andy Huelsebusch**. Sound: **Jim Calciano**. Music: **Charles Nieland**. Hoof effects: **Craig Lindberg**. Mower and make-up effects: **Ethan Reiff, Barry Sherman, Jim Gonis**.

RUNNING TIME:
**12 mins**

# King on TV

*Lock the door, switch on the set — and settle down for a cosy evening with your old chum — TERROR*

■ Richard Hagstrom has inherited an 'ultimate reality' word processor. Before it blows up, he 'enters' into his life a sack of gold, the 'idea' of 20 best-selling novels, and the woman and child he has always loved.

**Stephen King's** name first came up on the TV screen when *SALEM'S LOT* was produced as a two-part mini-series in 1979 (see pages 84-87). No further TV adaptations were embarked upon until 1985 when George A. Romero and Richard Rubinstein of Laurel Entertainment decided to branch out into TV with a series entitled *TALES FROM THE DARKSIDE*. Episodes of the series were characterized by a macabre humour; most of them had a 'twist'; and many concerned people's experiences with the 'other world'.

King suggested one of his stories (now in the *Skeleton Crew* collection) to Romero for *TALES FROM THE DARKSIDE*. Thus *WORD PROCESSOR OF THE GODS*, adapted by Michael McDowell, appeared in the first series, directed by Michael Gornick, who had been director of photography on many of Romero's films.

*WORD PROCESSOR OF THE GODS* is a wonderful fantasy tale. Richard Hagstrom, failed writer, husband and father, suddenly inherits a word processor which, when he types commands into its keyboards, executes them *literally*. Thus, Hagstrom is able to 'delete' his harridan of a wife and obnoxious son, and 'enter' instead his dream family. (Yes, this story does have a happy ending!)

*TALES FROM THE DARKSIDE* proved very popular and lasted for many years. Stephen King's next contribution to it was an original teleplay, *SORRY, RIGHT NUMBER* (1987). Katie Weiderman is the wife of a successful horror-novelist, William Weiderman. He hasn't been feeling very well lately. Katie is discussing his health in a phone call to her sister Lois when the other phone rings and Katie hears a distraught woman garbling incoherently. That night William dies.

Ten years later, a memory triggers Katie into a replay of that evening, and she discovers she was the woman caller, ringing from the future, trying to warn her 'young' self that her husband is dangerously ill.

In 1984/85, a new series of Rod Sterling's classic *THE TWILIGHT ZONE* series went into production. The

author Harlan Ellison (an old friend of King's) came in as a creative consultant, and was asked to do a script for King's story 'Gramma', now in his *Skeleton Crew* collection.

The story recaptured the frightening moment in King's childhood when he found the body of his dead grandmother. In *GRAMMA* (1987), 11-year-old George has, in an emergency, to look after his seriously ill grandmother — who has dabbled in evil things in her time. He brings her a cup of tea, even though he realizes the danger of entering her room. He thinks that she has died until she says his name — but her voice is 'dead'. By the time his mother gets home, his spirit has gone... stolen by his grandmother.

Bradford May made a nice job of *GRAMMA*. There is an eerie scene in which George's shadow is sucked into his grandmother's room. And there are some splendid camera movements, courtesy of recently developed Cam-

Remote equipment: the camera circles round George in the kitchen, constantly changes elevation as it tracks with him down the hallway, and then spins away from him as he reaches her bedroom.

In 1990, the magnificently brooding saga of *IT* went out on TV screens as a two-part, four-hour mini-series. It was followed by a frightening tale of some vengeful ghosts, *SOMETIMES THEY COME BACK* (1991), taken from a story in the *Night Shift* collection. Then came King's own original teleplay for the eight-part series *GOLDEN YEARS* (1991), which was a story about the terrifying aftermath of a government secret experiment which goes wrong. (See pages 88-93 for further details of those three productions).

Stephen King has also had many invitations to host *THE STEPHEN KING PLAYHOUSE*, the *NIGHT SHIFT* and other similar horror/sci-fi series, but he hasn't been tempted yet.

■ George is terrified of entering his grandmother's room. He knows that his soul is in serious danger because Gramma's going to take it, so that she doesn't have to die.

**The Films of Stephen King**

# Salem's Lot 1979

*Jerusalem's Lot, a nice little town in Maine — but don't go out after sundown...*

DIRECTOR:
**Tobe Hooper**
*(USA, 1979)*

CBS-TV: Two-part mini-series

LEADING PLAYERS:
**David Soul** (Ben Mears), **James Mason** (Straker), **Lance Kerwin** (Mark Petrie), **Bonnie Bedelia** (Susan Norton), **Lew Ayres** (Jason Burke), **Julie Cobb** (Bonnie Sawyer), **Elisha Cook** (Weasel), **George Dzundas** (Cully Sawyer), **Ed Flanders** (Dr Bill Norton), **Clarissa Kaye** (Marjorie Glick), **Geoffrey Lewis** (Mike Ryerson), **Barney McFadden** (Ned Tebbets), **Reggie Nalder** (Barlow), **Fred Willard** (Larry Crockett), **Kenneth McMillan** (Parkins Gillespie), **Marie Windsor** (Eva), **Brad Savage** (Danny Glick), **Ronnie Scriber** (Ralphie Glick).

PRODUCTION COMPANY:
**Warner Bros**

PRODUCER:
**Richard Kobritz**

TELEPLAY:
**Paul Monash**; based on the novel by **Stephen King**.

Photographer: **Jules Brenner**. Editor: **Carroll Sax**. Production designer: **Mort Rabinowitz**. Music: **Harry Sukman**. Special effects: **Frank Torro**. Special make-up: **Jack Young**. Colour.

RUNNING TIME:
Original mini-series: **210 mins**; TV movie: **150 mins**; European theatrical release: **112 mins**.

## SYNOPSIS

**P**ROLOGUE: In a small Central American town, a writer, Ben Mears, recalls his near escape from living death in his home town of Jerusalem's Lot in Maine.

FLASHBACK: Ben has returned to 'Salem's Lot to write a novel. He learns that the local 'haunted' house, the Marsten House, has recently been purchased by two antique dealers called Straker and Barlow. Mears begins to renew old acquaintances and establish new ones — especially with the lovely Susan Norton. He meets Straker, and finds him courteous but disquietingly sinister.

A mysterious crate is delivered to the Marsten House and put in the basement. It is the vampire Barlow's coffin. Straker kills town youngster Ralphie Glick to provide sustenance for Barlow. Ralphie becomes a vampire and returns to 'win over' his brother Danny. Another boy, Mark Petrie, then has a near escape from Danny. Shortly afterwards, Barlow pays a lethal visit to Mark's parents.

Dr Norton, Susan's father, and Mears set off to destroy Barlow. However, Susan and Mark have been caught by Straker. Ben manages to kill him and rescue Mark, but it's too late to save Susan. Ben and Mark find Barlow's coffin and drive a stake through his heart. They are surrounded by the town's undead, but Ben sets fire to the evil Marsten House and the vampires are destroyed in the flames.

EPILOGUE: Ben and Mark have been followed to their hideaway by the undead Susan. Ben, with much heartache, has to kill her with a stake. He warns Mark that there may still be others...

'**T**here will always be a special cold place in my heart for '*Salem's Lot*,' said Stephen King of his second published novel. 'It seemed to capture some of the special things about living in a small town that I'd known all my life'.

For Jerusalem's Lot, Maine, the location scouts chose Ferndale in northern California, which had previously proved successful as a 'Maine' movie town. However, nowhere could they find a stand-in for the Marsten House, so production designer Mort Rabinowitz and his team settled down to build it. They found a cottage that provided a central core for their edifice, and paid the cottage owners $20,000 for the 'inconvenience'.

## SALEM'S LOT: THE MOVIE

A theatrical version of *SALEM'S LOT* for European cinemas was planned from the outset. It did mean condensing King's tale down even more tightly (to 112 mins), but it wasn't subject to all of TV's restrictions. In the mini-series, for instance, the stake had to enter a vampire's heart off-camera; while Bill Norton's impaling on a wall of antler trophies retained far more gory detail for the movie version.

Nevertheless, director Tobe Hooper did achieve a couple of TV 'breakthroughs'. Hitherto it had not been permissible to show young children in situations of 'mortal jeopardy' on TV. Perhaps the Standards & Practices officials didn't believe in vampires, and so didn't believe the kids in *SALEM'S LOT* to be in any real danger. However, Hooper also managed to convince them that there was a difference between dead and 'undead'. This was an important achievement, because it was not permissible to show a corpse on TV with its eyes open; 'resting' vampires could, however, be filmed open-eyed.

Rabinowitz reckoned that it cost a further $100,000 to construct the exterior facades, and $70,000 to build the interiors back at Burbank Studios.

Producer Richard Kobritz felt that the Marsten House ought to be the 'rotting embodiment of the vampire's soul'; therefore the $70,000 wasn't even spent on making the place look good. Tons of plaster were used, so that craters and pock-marks could make every surface look rotten and sick, and an epoxy resin was 'dripped' from the cracks and crevices, as if the walls were oozing pus.

It created a satisfactory shock, therefore, when Straker, Barlow's 'business partner' — a character personified as the epitome of cold, courteous elegance by James Mason — transports himself around the suppurating building as if it were the most fastidious and gracious of living abodes.

Rabinowitz recalls how, on the night before shooting began, when they were working late trying to get everything finished, a car drove past, braked hard and then backed up. The driver got out and stared at the house in disbelief. 'My God,' he said, 'I've lived here 25 years and I never noticed that house before.'

The movie's main monster — Barlow — was the other subject on which producer Kobritz had strong feelings. Stephen King described him as 'strong and intelligent and handsome in a sharp, forbidding way'; he had swept-back hair and was immaculately tailored. Kobritz was tired of glamorous Count Draculas, and wanted to create '... a really unattractive, horrible-looking Barlow. We went back to the old [1922] German *NOSFERATU* concept where he is the essence of evil... The other thing we did with the character... is that Barlow does not speak... What kind of voice do you put behind a vampire?'

## KING ON SALEM'S LOT

*'The major emotion that went through my mind as I watched [SALEM'S LOT] was relief...'*

*'Most of what television touches within the horror genre turns out to be absolute drivel. I think [producer] Richard Kobritz and Tobe Hooper made SALEM'S LOT rise well above that. It certainly wasn't typical of horror movies made for television.'*

■ Little Ralphie Glick, one of the vampire Barlow's victims, has come back to the bedroom window to 'claim' his brother Danny. A special harness on the end of a crane was used for Ralphie's levitation, enabling him to 'float' very convincingly.

■ *Right*: Straker (left), Barlow (right) and Ben Mears (centre) in the Marsten House — the vampire's stronghold.
■ *Below*: Ben Mears, with a hastily improvised cross, keeps watch over one of the town's undead.

This decision brought forth one of King's few complaints about the mini-series, 'I didn't particularly approve of them turning Barlow into a sort of Nosferatu, who says nothing at all... That's a different concept than mine altogether, and I think it's one that's a little bit empty.'

Richard Kobritz was very involved with every aspect of *SALEM'S LOT*. It was he who rescued the project from the doldrums in Warner Bros. feature-films department, and brought it into the television section, where he was in charge of production. It was he who determined on Tobe Hooper as the mini-series' director. He spent a lot of time viewing horror films, and in the end decided that the director of *THE TEXAS CHAINSAW MASSACRE* (1974) was the man for him, 'I try to see every movie I can, try to come up with somebody who is young... I'm looking for somebody who is visual, who isn't wasting his time worrying about the politics of what the [film] unions are doing — that's my job.'

## A RETURN TO SALEM'S LOT

Horror-film director Larry Cohen (and scriptwriter for *CARRIE* (1986)) had long been interested in the goings-on in *SALEM'S LOT*. He had written a screenplay (not used) for the original movie, and now, in 1987, found himself back there again — this time story-writing, script-writing and directing. Stephen King had no connection with this film — apart from the name of the town and the fact of its vampire inhabitants.

Cohen's story had Joe Weber (played by Michael Moriarty), an anthropologist, and his son Jeremy (Ricky Addison Reed) 'lured' to 'Salem's Lot — as is explained by the community's leader, Judge Axel (Andrew Duggan) — to write a history of the vampire race and tell how they fled from persecution in Europe. Vampirism here is an unhidden, matter-of-fact way of life. Humans are 'kept' to look after the coffins. They are not used much for blood (cows are preferred) because they tend to heroin addiction and are an AIDS hazard. Jeremy decides he wants to be a vampire and his vampire girlfriend, Cathy (Katja Crosby), gets pregnant...

Although the vampires of *SALEM'S LOT* all seem to be satisfactorily despatched, with the help of Dr Van Meer (Samuel Fuller), at the film's end, the title *'A' RETURN...* could well mean it's not all over yet.

Kobritz had strong views about the casting, too. David Soul's initial attraction was his current TV popularity in the series *STARSKY AND HUTCH*, but both Kobritz and Hooper were very pleased with his performance. Getting James Mason for the role of Straker had been a 'coup'. Kobritz had hoped the Englishman might be available, that he might like the material, and that he might consider a television role — and he did. 'We were fortunate,' said Kobritz, '... he gives it so much of himself — he's such a classy actor.'

■ Only just in time, before the sun goes down, Ben and Mark find Barlow's coffin and they stake the vampire. And so the evil of 'Salem's Lot has been vanquished... or has it?

## The Films of Stephen King

# It 1990

DIRECTOR:
**Tommy Lee Wallace**
*(USA, 1990)*

ABC-TV: Two-part mini-series

LEADING PLAYERS:
**Harry Anderson** (Richie Tozier), **Dennis Christopher** (Eddie Kaspbrak), **Richard Masur** (Stan Uris), **Annette O'Toole** (Beverly Marsh), **Tim Reid** (Mike Hanlon), **John Ritter** (Ben Hanscom), **Richard Thomas** (Bill Denbrough), **Tim Curry** (Pennywise), **Jonathan Brandis** (young Bill), **Brandon Crane** (young Ben), **Adam Faraizl** (young Eddie), **Seth Green** (young Richie), **Ben Heller** (young Stan), **Emily Perkins** (young Bev), **Marlon Taylor** (young Mike), **Olivia Hussey** (Audra), **Sheila Moore** (Mrs Kaspbrak), **Jarred Blancard** (young Henry Bowers), **Michael Cole** (Henry Bowers), **Drum Garrett** (Belch Huggins), **Gabe Khouth** (Patrick Hockstetter), **Caitlin Hicks** (Patti Uris), **Tony Dakota** (Georgie Denbrough), **Terence Kelly** (Officer Nell).

PRODUCTION COMPANY:
**Green-Epstein Productions and Konigsberg/Sanitsky Productions** in association with **Lorimar Television.**

EXECUTIVE PRODUCERS:
**Jim Green, Allen Epstein**

TELEPLAY:
**Lawrence D. Cohen** (Parts 1 and 2), **Tommy Lee Wallace** (Part 2); based on the novel by **Stephen King.**

Photographer: **Richard Leiterman.**
Editors: **Robert F. Shugrue, David Blangsted.**
Production designer: **Douglas Higgins.**
Art director: **Eric Fraser.**
Music: **Richard Bellis.**

*IT knows.*
*IT waits.*
*IT kills.*

## SYNOPSIS

**PART 1**

Derry, Maine; 1990. A little girl — the sixth in recent months — has just been brutally murdered. Librarian Mike Hanlon calls up six childhood friends to tell them that the time has come to return to Derry to honour a promise they made 30 years ago.

The friends are now scattered far and wide. Bill Denbrough is a horror novelist as well as being a scriptwriter; Ben Hanscom is now an award-winning architect; Beverly March a successful fashion designer; Eddie Kaspbrak the owner of a fleet of limousines; Stan Uris a businessman in Atlanta; Richie Tozier a famous comedian. Their year of childhood horror began when It, appearing in the form of Pennywise, the grinning but extremely malevolent clown, ripped an arm off Bill's little brother Georgie, who then died. Many murders and manifestations followed, and the kids banded themselves together as The Losers' Club. They thought they had killed It then, but swore they would return if he ever reappeared; and he's back.

**PART 2**

The Losers' Club begins to arrive in Derry — all except Stan, who slit his wrists after the phone call. Each of them has a terrifying encounter

■ All those of The Loser's Club who are still alive and fighting fit have descended into the sewer tunnels below the town of Derry for their final confrontation with the creature known as It. There, Bill discovers that his wife Audra is It's prisoner.

with Pennywise, including Bill's wife Audra, who followed him to Derry and is now It's prisoner. It marshals its forces. Mike is attacked and hospitalized. The remaining five head for the sewers, It's hiding place, and finally encounter It in its most ferocious manifestation — a huge spidery monster. Eddie is fatally wounded by the creature, but Bev manages to shoot It and then Bill rips out It's heart.

Audra is rescued, Mike slowly recovers in hospital, and Derry becomes, once again, just another little town in Maine.

*IT* **is the small-screen** adaptation of one of Stephen King's biggest and most popular books. It was, literally, a mammoth undertaking to get it all into four hours minus all the time out for commercials. However, Larry (Lawrence D.) Cohen and Tommy Lee Wallace have succeeded in leaving out nothing which weakens the central story line — that of the seven brave Losers' two-fold battle with It.

Larry Cohen (already, at this time, acclaimed for his script for *CARRIE* (1976)) said, 'Part of my interest in *IT*, and my pleasure in it, is that Steve [King] has an uncanny gift for writing about kids... He has a gift for creating what childhood and adolescence are like, not really *recreating* it.'

It is an extraordinarily evil power. It is an unfathomable, unnameable creature. It rubs raw wounds, deep within. It is a hellish force, capable of turning itself into the worst nightmares of those it will destroy. It gains strength from their fear. It wages an underground war — both in the sewers of Derry, and in the emotions and the memories of those it wishes to annihilate. It is the cruelty of every parent, the betrayal of every friend, the guilt of every broken promise.

But It hadn't reckoned on The Loser's Club — seven plucky kids who realise that by sticking together, through thick and thin, by believing they can win, and by refusing to be fooled or swayed by It's tricks and torments, they can defeat It.

As personified by Tim Curry's Pennywise, the menacing clown, cackling with evil glee, the fear that has to be faced is bone-chilling. As personified by Fantasy 2's chicken-wire-framed spider monster, It lacks a certain awesomeness. Nevertheless, the last half-hour apart, *IT* should warm the hearts of King fans everywhere.

Costume designer: **Monique Stranan**. Special-effects make-up: **Bart K. Mixon**. Special visual-effects supervisor: **Gene Warren Jnr** (Fantasy 2).

RUNNING TIME: **240 mins** (including commercials)

■ Pennywise the clown. A terrifying mass of colour around a deathly chalk-white face and a cackle of evil glee signify that It is in murderous mood and has once again shape-shifted into human form.

The Films of
Stephen King

DIRECTOR:
**Tom McLoughlin**
*(1991, USA)*

CBS-TV movie

LEADING PLAYERS:
**Tim Matheson** (Jim
Norman), **Brooke Adams**
(Sally Norman), **Robert
Rusler** (Lawson), **Chris
Demetral** (Wayne Norman),
**Robert Hy Gorman** (Scott
Norman), **William
Sanderson** (Mueller),
**Nicholas Sadler** (Vinnie),
**Bentley Mitchum** (North),
**Matt Nolan** (Billy), **Tasia
Valenza** (Kate), **Chadd
Nyerges** (Chip), **T. Max
Graham** (Chief Pepper),
**William Kuhlke** (Principal
Simpson), **Duncan McLeod**
(old Officer Nell), **Nancy
McLoughlin** (Dr Bernardi),
**Zachary Ball** (Jimmy
Norman), **Don Ruffin** (young
Mueller), **Kimball Gimmings**
(young Officer Nell).

PRODUCTION COMPANY:
**Come Back Productions**

PRODUCER:
**Michael S. Murphy**

CO-PRODUCER
**Milton Subotsky**

SCREENPLAY:
**Lawrence Konner, Mark
Rosenthal**; based on the
short story by **Stephen
King**, from the *Night Shift*
collection.

Photographer: **Bryan
England**. Editor: **Charles
Bornstein**. Production
designer: **Philip Dean
Foreman**. Art Director:
**Timothy R. Bauer**.

# Sometimes They Come Back 1991

*If Jim had known the
horror he was facing —
he wouldn't have come back*

## SYNOPSIS

Jim Norman, with his wife Sally and son Scott, leaves Chicago to take up a high-school teaching post at the Harold Davis High School in his home town of Stratford, Connecticut. In Stratford, when he was nine-years-old, Jim had witnessed the murder of his 11-year-old brother, Wayne, by a gang of thugs in a railway tunnel. Jim ran away; but the three louts didn't move fast enough and were mown down by the oncoming train.

Now, at Davis High, Jim's favourite pupils are being inexplicably murdered. As each disappears, a 'new' pupil turns up in his place. Jim recognises them as the boys who killed his brother — and whom he knows to be buried in the local cemetery.

These murderous ghosts are angry with Jim. They want him to relive the night of his brother's death, this time without running away. What Jim hasn't yet remembered is that his running away was directly responsible for their death. The thug ghouls threaten Jim and his family. Come the final showdown in the old, now-closed, railway tunnel, Jim cries out to Wayne for help. Wayne's spirit appears, and now Jim doesn't run away but stays and fights. A ghost train rushes out of the darkness, and this time the ghouls are smashed to eternal smithereens.

**U**ndeterred by the lack of blockbuster success for some of his five previous collaborations with Stephen King, and by the closure of his North Carolina studios, movie-mogul Dino De Laurentiis moved back, full-blast, into production. He was at this point concentrating on making films for US television which were then theatrically released elsewhere in the world. And De Laurentiis still had in his possession the control of several of King's stories, including 'Sometimes They Come Back' from the *Night Shift* collection. The recent success of *IT* (1990) as a TV mini-series meant that

Sound: **Mark Bovos**.
Music: **Terry Plumeri**.
Costume designer: **Karen Patch**. Make-up: **Daniel Marc, Patti Brand**.
Special-effects make-up: **Gabe Bartalos; Atlantic West Effects**.
Special-effects co-ordinator: **Marty Bresin**.
Stunt co-ordinator: **Rick Baker**. Colour: **DeLuxe**.

RUNNING TIME:
**97 mins**

CBS-TV executives were enthusiastic about putting more of King's stories on the small screen.

Signed to direct SOMETIMES THEY COME BACK was Tom McLoughlin, whose previous films had ranged from ghoulish horror, in bringing Jason back from the grave (again) in FRIDAY THE 13TH: JASON LIVES (1986), to comic fantasy in DATE WITH AN ANGEL (1987), with French star Emmanuelle Beart as his ethereally beautiful, broken-winged cherub.

McLoughlin was equally undeterred by the idea of being associated with another Stephen King movie, 'I'm much more honoured than intimidated,' he said. He believed that he and King were part of a generation — which included Steven Spielberg and George Lucas — that '...all had much the same childhood. We were all shaped by the same influences. So I can see where King is coming from. And I can appreciate King's genius for reinterpreting and drawing on those common influences.'

The director set out with the intention of producing a movie that would appeal to a wide audience without upsetting Stephen King fans. However, because it was a TV movie, there was a limit to how many stomach-turning scenes could be included. The shocks and scares had to be done far more with acting than with splatter-packed special-effects. Nevertheless, Gabe Bartalos's make-up for the back-from-the-grave troublemakers is satisfyingly gory, for those times when they are in

lethal humour, and superbly pale and ominous when they're just threatening.

Changes were made in transferring story to screen. One of the less happy outcomes is that Jim's return to Stratford and his catapulting into occult chaos doesn't allow time to get one's bearings. There is a hint, near the end, that the ghouls have planned it all to coincide with the anniversary of their 'death'. Otherwise, no clue is given as to why Jim should return to such a den of childhood trauma.

In King's *Night Shift* story, Jim's wife is murdered by the 'ghosts', though not in the film, but the film gives Jim a son, Scott, whom he didn't have before. Through his love for Scott, Jim attempts to recreate the special relationship that died with his brother Wayne, and to assuage the guilt that he felt on running away. The film wants Jim to be able to do a great deal more than crush the evil spectres that personify his remorse; it offers him a tough passage and a cathartic climax — but a happy future.

■ All his life, Jim Norman has been haunted by the memory of the three teenage thugs who murdered his brother. Now their three very solid and very nasty ghosts have appeared, with their own reasons for forcing a replay of the murder night.

■ Sally Norman doesn't know why her husband has come back to Derry. All she knows is that he's close to a nervous breakdown, and that a sinister black car keeps driving past the house.

**The Films of Stephen King**

# Golden Years 1991

DIRECTORS:
**Kenneth Fink, Allen Coulter, Michael G. Gornick, Stephen Tolkin.**
*(USA, 1991)*

CBS-TV: Seven-part mini-series

LEADING PLAYERS:
**Keith Szarabajka** (Harlan Williams), **Felicity Huffman** (Terry Spann), **Frances Sternhagen** (Gina Williams), **Ed Lauter** (General Louis Crewes), **R.D. Call** (Jude Andrews), **Bill Raymond** (Dr Richard Todhunter), **Matt Malloy** (Redding), **Adam Redfield** (Jackson), **John Rothman** (Dr Ackerman), **Stephen Root** (Major Moreland), **J.R. Horne** (Dr Eakins), **Graham Paul** (Rick Haverford), **Peter McRobbie** (Lt McGiver), **Phil Lenkowsky** (Billy DeLois), **Brad Greenquist** (Steven Dent), **Mert Hatfield** (Sheriff Mayo), **Michael P. Moran** (the trucker), **Stephen King** (the bus driver), **Josef Anderson** (the janitor), **Sarah Melici** (Mrs Rogers), **Randell Haynes** (Yaniger), **Harriet Samson Harris** (Francie Williams), **Peter McIntosh** ('Shop' Commander), **Jeff Williams** (Lt Vester), **Jonathan Teague Cook** (Cap'n Trips), **Paul Butler** (Captain Marsh), **Lili Bernard** (Harlan's nurse).

PRODUCTION COMPANY:
**Laurel Entertainment Inc.**

PRODUCERS:
**Mitchell Galin, Peter McIntosh**

TELEPLAY:
**Stephen King** (first five episodes), **Josef Anderson** (last two episodes); story idea created by **Stephen King**.

*For Harlan, growing old wasn't a problem: he was growing younger*

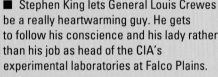

## SYNOPSIS

The fall-out from an explosion caused by a botched experiment contaminates Harlan Williams, an elderly janitor at Falco Plains government experimental lab, and he begins to grow younger. Kindly government agent Terry Spann realizes that Harlan and his wife Gina may be in danger from the 'Shop', a sinister government agency, and the three of them decide to leave town. 'Shop' agent Jude Andrews takes over Falco Plains and begins hunting for Harlan — and Terry — with whom he has old scores to settle. Terry's boss (and partner), General Louis Crewes, hides Harlan's files from Andrews and then sets out to help Terry.

The escaping trio decide to take separate routes. Harlan's symptoms are escalating. He grows younger daily, radiates a green glow, and causes electrical disturbances and earthquakes. Gina, now health-threatened by all the stress, and Terry go to the Williams' blind

■ Stephen King lets General Louis Crewes be a really heartwarming guy. He gets to follow his conscience and his lady rather than his job as head of the CIA's experimental laboratories at Falco Plains.

daughter, Francie, in Chicago. Harlan soon joins them, followed first by Louis Crewes, and then by Andrews with armed guards.

After a series of near-miss escapes from the 'Shop', Terry, Louis, Harlan and Gina head out into open countryside. Once again Andrews is right behind them, but this time Terry shoots and kills him. Harlan finds himself bathed in a strange light. He realizes his time has come; he puts his arms around Gina and they 'combust' in a flash together. Terry and Louis go off into the sunset.

**How much younger** can you comfortably get? This was the issue that deeply troubled Gina Williams (Frances Sternhagen with a part in another King story, after her role in *MISERY*). At 65, and feeling her age, she's having to watch her 70-year-old husband losing his grey hair and wrinkles, and displaying energy he hasn't

had for years. She has been trying to get Harlan to retire and look after his cabbages, and instead he finds a perky new lease of life.

Gina both worries about and resents the 'new' Harlan, and chooses to sink into the depths of terminal gloom. Before we know exactly what has befallen Harlan, there is a delightful scene where he and Gina make love in the hospital shower. Great stuff. But was such an elderly coupling only being permitted on screen because Harlan had shed a load of years on fall-out impact? Hopefully not.

Terry is a fascinating proposition (Terrilynn, according to her mom). This is a tough, cool, intelligent, sexy lady, and one who comes to find, in her depths, considerable care for others. Stephen King thought her up all by himself. She still has an interesting left-over relationship with the coldly vicious Jude Andrews. They were partners, and there was much mutual admiration until his professional practices took a grossly unacceptable turn. She hasn't forgiven him for being despicable; and he hasn't forgiven her for despising him.

Back to the experiments. These are the work of Dr Richard Todhunter, a mad boffin whose life's mission seems to be to stop mice from growing up; perhaps he's a baby-mouse molester. However, his scientific antics finally get right out of hand, and he and everything around him blow up.

The high point of Todhunter's experiments is how Nepomniaschy photographs them: Todhunter's black, basement, ultra-high-tech lab; his wild little face; and his surreal white mice — all are lit with a glow of excitement, a shimmer of terror, a frisson of fear.

*GOLDEN YEARS* was, too often, slow; the pacing slipped at many points. There were too many meaningful pauses after meaningful lines; Stephen King tended to let words get the upper hand. And events from Chicago onward were cluttered. Francie was too complex a character for the time allowed her, and the hippie-commune hideaway was a mystifying inclusion. The scary elements were those of a thriller — high-tension chases, heartless assailants — while the sci-fi ingredients were rather benign and woolly. It was originally written with a cliffhanger ending, leaving the door open for more episodes, but minds changed and a closing scene was written and filmed. Whatever further adventures may have been lost — it was a satisfying, uplifting ending.

Photographer: **Alex Nepomniaschy**. Editors: **Richard Harkness, Michael Kewley, Stephen Mark**. Production designer: **Jeremy Conway**. Art director: **Kim Jennings**. Sound: **Felipe Borrero**. Music: **Joe Taylor**. Theme music: 'Golden Years': **David Bowie**. Costume designer: **Gilda Texter**. Special make-up consultant: **Dick Smith**. Harlan's make-up designers: **Carl Fullerton, Neal Martz**. Special effects: **Steve Kirshoff**. Stunt co-ordinators: **Jerry Hewitt, Danny Aiello III**. Technicolor.

RUNNING TIME: **Eight hours** (including commercials)

■ For the rejuvenating of Harlan, three sets of facial appliances were designed. It took make-up experts five hours a day to apply them.

# In the Seedbed

■ In *THE TOMMY-KNOCKERS*, a TV mini-series, Jimmy Smits plays Jim Gardener, the man who discovers that the quiet little town of Haven has undergone some terrible changes.

***Don't get too comfortable. Even now, in a little back room somewhere, the next Stephen King movie is coming to life...***

**T**he 'in production' pages of cinema trade papers invariably indicate that a 'King' movie is germinating or sprouting somewhere. A couple of interesting ones put out shoots, but then fell by the wayside. One was *THE SHOTGUNNERS*, from an original script by King, which was offered to the director Sam Peckinpah. It was a strange story of vigilante ghosts from the last century appearing in a Western town to avenge a hanging. They came, not on horseback, but in three long, black Cadillacs with darkened windows. Peckinpah was in pre-production when, in 1984, he died of a heart attack. King says it's one of his favourite pieces of work, and he cannot understand why nobody else has shown any interest in the project.

*APT PUPIL*, from a novella in King's *Different Seasons* collection, was put into production by Richard Kobritz in 1988. It was being directed by Alan Bridges when, after ten weeks of shooting, the film ran out of money. It looked as if the film's backers found the story unpalatable, but no definite explanation was given. It tells of Todd Bowden (played by Ricky Schroder), an all-American 13-year-old, who discovers a Nazi war criminal, Kurt Dussander (Nicol Williamson), is living in his Californian hometown, and becomes an active pupil of the Nazi's murderous skills.

*THE TOMMYKNOCKERS* was, in 1993, adapted as a TV mini-series by Larry Cohen (who previously scripted *CARRIE* (1976) and *IT* (1990)). Shot in

JIMMY SMITS    MARG HELGENBERGER

Something wonderful is happening in Haven.

Pray it doesn't happen to you.

STEPHEN KING'S
THE TOMMYKNOCKERS

ABC World Premiere Event   Sunday, May 9   9/8 C   abc

New Zealand by director John Power, it is the story of Bobbi Anderson, a writer living in the small town of Haven, Maine, who unwittingly unleashes the powers of Tommyknockers when she digs up a piece of metal which turns out to be a spaceship. The Tommyknockers 'take over' Bobbi and the other inhabitants of Maine, feeding them with high-level technological know-how which they will later turn to their own ends. The only one resistant to their power is Bobbi's alcoholic poet friend Jim Gardener, played in the movie by Jimmy Smits. Also in the cast are Robert Carradine, Marg Helgenberger and Traci Lords.

George A. Romero was, for a long time, keen to direct *THE STAND*, and wrote a screenplay which, said King, was great, but far too long. However, King's epic fantasy went into production in 1993 as another TV mini-series, this time directed by Mick Garris (of *SLEEPWALKERS* (1993)).

Castle Rock Entertainment is developing *RITA HAYWORTH AND THE SHAWSHANK REDEMPTION*, from a novella in King's *Different Seasons* collection. Andy, a lifer in Shawshank Penitentiary, has acquired a poster of Rita Hayworth. Rita's job is to hide the hole Andy is chipping through his cell wall. The film stars Tim Robbins, Morgan Freeman and Brad Pitt. Castle Rock, who have first rights on all new King material, have also acquired his chilling novel *Dolores Claiborne*.

Plans for *THE TALISMAN*, based on the epic fantasy novel co-authored by Stephen King and Peter Straub, are still being discussed. Both King and Straub are very keen that Steven Spielberg should involve himself in this project.

Richard Rubinstein's Laurel Entertainment has been working on *NIGHT FLIER*, possibly as a two-hour TV movie, an adaptation of a story in the *Prime Evil* anthology. Dwight Renfield is a modern-day vampire who flies by means of a plane: he's a pilot who spends the daylight hours asleep in his cargo hold. He's up against Richard Dees, a reporter for the *Inside View* tabloid, who's trying to solve a series of ghoulish airport murders.

*THINNER* (by 'Richard Bachman') is in development at Laurel Entertainment, with a script by Michael McDowell, and with Tom Holland pencilled in as director. It is the terrifying tale of a seriously tubby lawyer, Bill Halleck, who, after incurring a gypsy's wrath, begins to lose weight — and can't stop. King has said his choice for Halleck would be John Candy. Laurel are also tinkering with the idea of *THE LANGOLIERS* (a novella from his *Four Past Midnight* collection), and *TALES FROM THE DARKSIDE: THE MOVIE 2*. And Tobe Hooper, the director of *SALEM'S LOT*, has been working on the *Night Shift* story 'The Mangler'.

And the next Stephen King film to be announced… will probably be the next one he writes.

■ *Dolores Claiborne*, which was under consideration for a movie adaptation even before it had reached the bookshelves.

# Index

## PICTURE CREDITS

t=top  b=bottom
Via British Film Institute:
10,13{b},16,18,24,25{b},26,30,31{b},
32,33{b},35{t},38,43,50,
53,54,57,60{t},64,66,69,70.
Castle Rock Entertainment: 68,78,79.
CBS TV: 83,90.
Columbia Pictures: 72.
Columbia Tristar International:
75,76{both},77.
De Laurentiis Corp.: 28,41.
Hodder & Stoughton: 80,95.
International Film Corp.: 44.
JAC Publicity: 91{both}.
Kobal Collection:
7,8,9{t},12,13{t},14,15,
17{both},19,22{both},23,25{t},29,31{t},
33{t},34,35{b},36,37,39,40,42,45,46,
49,51,52,53,58,59,60{b},61,62,63,
65,67,73,86{t},88,89,Back cover.
Laurel Entertainment: 20,82.
Moviestore Collection: 11{b},21,92,93.
Orion Pictures: 74.
Ronald Grant Archive: 6,11{t},27,55,56.
Shooting Star: 9{b},47,48,85,86{b},87,94.
Warner Brothers: 84 .
Wonderland Entertainment: 81.

Every effort has been made to trace the copyright holders of this material and we apologise for any omissions.